COLLEGE
APOLOGETICS

COLLEGE
APOLOGETICS

BY

REV. ANTHONY F. ALEXANDER

DEPARTMENT OF RELIGION

JOHN CARROLL UNIVERSITY

*And he saw . . . a ladder standing upon the
earth, and the top thereof touching heaven.*

GENESIS 28:12.

HENRY REGNERY COMPANY
CHICAGO

Nihil Obstat. Very Rev. Edward L. Hughes, O.P.,
Censor Librorum.
Imprimatur. ✠ Samuel Cardinal Stritch, D.D.,
Archiepiscopus Chicagiensis.
October 13, 1953.

Preface

THE PURPOSE of a university is to promote the discovery of truth and to inspire and direct the quest of wisdom, to achieve a higher education in harmony with the ideals of Christian Humanism. To attain this goal it must conserve, interpret, and transmit the knowledge, ideas, and values of our Christian heritage. It must, to be sure, extend the frontiers of knowledge through investigation, scholarly research, and the proper publication of this achievement. It must keep professional preparation on a broad and solid basis which will insure that the principles underlying different professions are understood and appreciated. It must give due and proper regard to the physical and mental health of its students. But it must do more.

A true university should maintain not only a standard but also a hierarchy of values. It must place humane above material values; and supernatural values above the merely humane. A university that lives up to the finest tradition of Christian humanism believes that its ideal product is "the supernatural man who thinks, judges, and acts constantly and consistently in accordance with right reason illumined by the supernatural light of the example and teaching of Christ."

Our understanding of truth, wisdom, and Christian humanism, our formation of a true sense of educational values, must look to every source of knowledge for assistance. It must use the best that science has to offer. It must look to the finest attainments of human reason as represented by philosophy. But it must also look to revelation.

While the great body of philosophical and scientific knowledge was being built up through human efforts over the course of history to attain objective truth, God was at the same time revealing truth to men, a bit here and a bit there, through the succeeding prophets whom He sent to His chosen people. Last of all He granted the climax to this rich endowment through His Son, Jesus Christ, Who came to earth not only to redeem the human race but also to teach it how to live.

Theology is the science that studies the body of truth that God has thus revealed. For this reason the university must look not only to the highest of the human sciences, philosophy, but also to the highest of all sciences, theology, for aid in its quest for a correct understanding of truth, wisdom, and true humanism, and for the construction of an objectively valid sense of values.

The very term *university* implies an all-embracing scope of activity. It must not only offer its services to the universe of men; it must also extend the area of its activity in research to the universe of knowable things, and it must seek that knowledge from every available source. It must look to natural science, to the arts which are crowned by the best in philosophy. But philosophy, art, and natural science give only partial answers to the world riddle. They give the human answer only. There are also divine answers, and those divine answers are found in theology. Theology, therefore, is an essential factor in humanistic education. If the university's unity of thought and purpose comes from its totality of outlook, then that totality must take in the whole science of theology. God and the supernatural must be the basis of its system of education: the true faith and the practice of that faith must be an integrating principle.

With this in mind it is not hard to see the place of apologetics in any adequate system of education. Philosophy gives us the best in human wisdom; theology explains to us divine wisdom itself. Apologetics, drawing its synthesis from the fields of philosophy and science, leads us to the very portals of faith by its conclusions. Only upon entering the portals of the temple of faith can we possess a true theology.

It is through the Theology Department that the university

seeks to impart to students a fuller understanding of the truths of revelation. It is through the specific courses in apologetics that the development of theology provides students with a ready knowledge of the reasonable arguments upon which their faith in these dogmas of revelation is founded. If this is done well, the way is open for the student to pursue with peace of mind and security of faith an ever greater knowledge of scientific theology. He can go on to study the social aspects of that theology in the Christian social order, and finally acquire a true appreciation of Catholicism as a culture embracing and supplementing all the fields of human activity.

A book such as *College Apologetics,* proceeding as it does with clarity, accuracy, and logical precision to build a truly solid bridge between reason and revelation, is a welcome instrument in the field of religious education. Father Alexander's successful career as a teacher, moreover, is added assurance that these qualities are joined in his book with a sure sense of the practicalities of the classroom. His rare combination of sound scholarship and effective presentation has been long proved with many university students directly under his care, and this incorporation into textbook form should provide a valuable extension of his work to an enlarged sphere of American and Catholic service.

VERY REV. FREDERICK E. WELFLE, S.J.
President, John Carroll University

Feast of All Saints, 1953

Contents

Contents

Charts and Tables

Part One

THE ORIGIN OF RELIGION

AN OUTLINE OF APOLOGETICS

Proofs for the existence of God.
Proofs for the existence of Soul.

The relationship between God and man engenders in man the obligation to practice religion.

Religion can be either ⎰ Natural
⎱ Supernatural

If supernatural revelation is a fact, then man cannot reject it in favor of tenets of natural religion.

Man must inquire into religions which claim to be agencies that impart to man the doctrines of supernatural revelation.

Christianity claims to be one of these religions.

The Gospels are said to be documents which furnish some of the credentials of Christianity.

Apart from inspiration, the Gospels can be pronounced trustworthy when inquiry is made into their ⎰ Integrity
⎱ Authorship
Historicity

The theme of the Gospels is Jesus Christ.

Christ appealed to His miracles and prophecies as furnishing authority for His mission and teaching.

Christ's miracles and prophecies do establish the truthfulness of His teaching for it can be proved to have God as their origin.

It follows that miracles and prophecies prove that Christ was what He claimed to be, namely God.

Since Christ is divine He has a good reason for all that He does.

One of Christ's reasons for coming to earth was to teach all men of all ages those things which they must

Do to be saved
Believe to be saved

Christ did not intend to remain on earth to do this teaching.

So that His doctrines would be transmitted to all men Christ founded a teaching agency called His Church.

To prevent anyone from making an error in finding the True Church, Christ impressed on it FOUR marks of identification.

Christ intended his Church to be

1—One in doctrine and government.
2—Holy in Founder, doctrine and members.
3—Universal in time and place.
4—Traceable to the person of Peter as its first ruler.

The Church which has these four marks and whose name corresponds to them is:

One
Holy
Catholic
Roman Church.

Since this Church was founded by Christ and endowed with His authority to teach, it follows that under certain conditions it is infallible when teaching and explaining matters pertaining to

Faith or what man must believe to be saved.
Morals or what man must do to be saved.

The Church using her infallible teaching authority has said that the fonts of divine revelation to men are:

Sacred Scripture or the Written Word of God.
Sacred Tradition or the Unwritten Word of God.

Act of Faith.

I

The Importance of Apologetics

Definition

THE WORD "apologetics" is derived from a Greek verb which means "to defend." An apology is usually a defense of an intellectual nature. It consists of the listing of the reasons for some particular course of action or for holding a certain belief. We shall see that in this book it has a more technical meaning.

The history of religious thought shows that there are two positions which have led to absurdity. They are faith without reason and reason without faith. It will be shown that truth is to be found in the position which holds that reason proves the fittingness and necessity of faith.

Before a religion can claim to speak with divine authority, it must prove that it was endowed with it by God. It cannot demand assent to its doctrines unless there is a solid basis for this faith. Before it speaks, it must present its credentials. If it demands faith without presenting these credentials, then it will be moving in a vicious circle for faith is believing on the authority of another.

The Christian Era was not very old when there appeared an error which will always remain as a good example of what can develop when a religion completely divorces faith from reason. Within a century after the death of Christ there appeared the error known as Gnosticism. Its devotees claimed to have a superior knowledge of religious matters but they could never prove their connection with the source of this "superior knowledge." They demanded blind faith of all who would join their sects. But since they had no touch-stone or rule by which they could periodically check on the truth of their doctrines, these Gnostics lost themselves in all sorts of vagaries. Their imaginations became the chief source of their tenets. St. Irenaeus said that by the latter part of the Second Century, there were over eighty of these sects in existence. What we have said of Gnosticism is true of almost all the religions of history which have insisted on faith in their doctrines without establishing a basis for this faith.

Opposite Gnosticism is the almost equally absurd position of rationalism which insists on reason without faith in religious matters. It holds that reason unaided by revelation is sufficient in discovering these truths. Regardless of a religion's validity or the authority of its proponents to teach, this error holds that every doctrine must pass the test of comprehensibility; if the inner nature of a mystery cannot be understood, then that doctrine must be rejected. This error makes divine revelation unnecessary.

The history of the pagan nations abundantly shows that, practically speaking, divine revelation is necessary if man is to learn the truths of even natural religion clearly, quickly and infallibly. Experience teaches that man cannot comprehend many things in the natural order and so he *a fortiori* cannot unaidedly discover truths of the supernatural order. Common sense tells us that since divine revelation in no way contradicts the nature of God Who makes it and the nature of man who receives it, it is fitting and possible.

To be assured of truth in matters of supernatural religion, there must be a combination of faith and reason. This union is not artificial but one demanded by the nature of the case and the testimony of human experience. An agency or an individual must present its credentials before it can claim to be God's mouthpiece and the validity of these credentials must be established by reason. Apologetics is the study in which we prove by reason that the Church is the agency set up by God to carry on His work of teaching the doctrines of supernatural religion. This branch of learning is defined as: *the rational science which establishes the teaching authority of the Roman Catholic Church as the rule of faith.*

Divisions

All the people of the world are divided into three main groups according to their religious convictions. It seems reasonable, therefore, to divide the treatment of apologetics into three parts. In each part we briefly discuss the truth or error of the convictions of one of these groups of people. When the three sections have been completed, the arguments for the teaching authority of the Church will have been outlined.

In the first subdivision of apologetics we discuss the reasons why men should hold that God exists and that the practice of religion is necessary. It will be shown that those who believe in the existence of God are logical in their convictions, while those who deny it *a fortiori* are not. The topics treated in this section are more or less of a philosophical nature. They are the arguments for the existence of God and the existence of a spiritual soul in man. An examination of the relationship which exists between the soul and God leads us to conclude that the practice of religion is of strict obligation. The section is concluded by calling attention to the fact that although man has the powers to arrive at the truths of natural religion, it is very difficult for most men to do so without the aid of supernatural revelation.

Since the conclusions of the first section of apologetics are so clear and cogent, it follows that those who deny them must be labeled illogical in their denials.

1. Those who deny the existence of God are atheists.

2. Those who deny the existence of a spiritual soul in man are materialists and positivists—they will admit the existence only of material things.

3. Those who deny the strict obligation to practice religion are called indifferentists.

4. The fourth group of those in error are rationalists who deny the necessity or possibility of God's making a supernatural revelation to man. They deny the truth of any religious doctrine which cannot be fully understood and so eliminate religious mysteries from the realm of possibility.

The **second** section of apologetics is devoted to the search for evidence of God's revelation to man. Let us examine the validity of Christianity first, for Christ claimed to impart to man the articles of divine revelation. We begin the inquiry by investigating the worth of the historical documents which are said to be the record of the beginnings of Christianity. Those documents are called the Gospels. Their trustworthiness is first proved and then they are examined. Their theme is Jesus Christ. The reason for the great emphasis on Christ in these writings is that He claimed and proved to be God. He came to earth for several reasons but the one which interests the student of apologetics is that He came to teach what all men must do and believe to be saved. He came, in short, to impart supernatural revelation to man.

After we prove what is stated in the preceding paragraph, it will be apparent that the true religion must be a Christian religion and that all non-Christian religions are wrong. The notable non-Christian religions of the world are Buddhism, Confucianism, Mohammedanism and Judaism. Their great age is absolutely no guarantee of their worth. If Christianity is true it is because it has authority to teach. These are wrong because they lack it. Even though they hold to the existence of God and the necessity of religion, the fundamental reason why they are wrong is that they refuse to accept Christ and His teachings.

In the **third** section of this study we attempt to determine whether or not all Christian religions are true. This inquiry will yield the following evidence. Christ intended that the doctrines which He taught be transmitted to all the races of people in the world from His time down to the end of the world. But He himself chose not to remain on earth to do this teaching. To carry out this task, He founded a teaching agency called His Church. But Christ foresaw that, in the centuries to come, there would arise wrong churches which would teach doctrines contrary to those taught by His Church. He could see that, in the conflict of teachings, the ordinary person would become confused and soon despair of finding the True Church. To protect the honest inquirer from making a mistake in finding the True Church, Christ impressed four identifying marks on it. The name of the True Church is derived from these four marks. It is the One, Holy, Catholic and Apostolic Church. Christ pronounced condemnation on all who refused to accept His teachings as they were taught by this Church. It teaches by divine authority and so God protects it from error in teaching doctrines which concern faith and morals.

Since none of the non-Catholic Christian sects have the four marks of identification which Christ impressed upon His Church, they are wrong and unauthorized. The principal non-Catholic Christian groups are made up of the Orthodox and Protestant sects.

The general conclusion which can be drawn after the discussion of the three parts of apologetics has been completed is that for one to be logical in the matter of religious belief, it is not enough simply to believe in God or be a follower of Christ. Besides this, one must also admit the authority of the Catholic Church as the rule of faith.

Mistaken Rules of Faith

From time to time in the ages past, wrong rules of faith have appeared. Some of them have persisted to the present day and have arrested the attention of many people. Since their proponents have been tireless in propagating their opinions, we deem it fitting to appraise each rule briefly.

1. Protestantism holds that the Bible alone, privately interpreted, is sufficient to point out what all must do and believe to be saved. It denies the existence of any divinely-appointed, living intermediary between God and man. It says that except for the Bible, man needs no outside help in discovering how God expects religion to be practiced. The reading of the Bible will teach all necessary truth.

In answer to this we say that the Bible is indeed God's inspired word and contains some of His revelation to man. The Church has always encouraged the reading of the Scriptures as a salutary practice. But there are several notable weaknesses in the Protestant position of the surpassing importance of the private interpretation of the Bible as a rule of faith.

a. It cannot be proved from the Bible itself or from any ancient Christian source that private interpretation of the Scriptures is the authentic rule of faith, nor can it be proved that the Bible is the sole vehicle of God's revelation to man.

b. Private interpretation of the Bible, upon which Protestants say salvation is contingent, was and is impossible for a great many people because they are illiterate. If an illiterate person accepts another's interpretation, then it is not his own private one.

c. Before one can interpret, he must understand. The average layman will find many parts of the Bible very difficult to understand. It was written from two to three thousand years ago in languages very different from our own, and filled with figures of speech, idiomata, and sentence structures which in many instances are almost impossible to translate literally. Any understanding of the Bible will be a superficial one unless the reader is well acquainted with the Oriental culture of most of the writers and with the political, social, and geographical factors which often color the narrative.

d. Those who hold that salvation rests upon the private interpretation of the whole Bible are forced to conclude that there was a time when Christians could not be saved because in their day the Bible was not yet completed. Christ died about the year 30 A.D. The first book of the New Testament to be written was probably St. Paul's First Epistle to the Thessalonians written about 51 A.D. and the last book written was St. John's Gospel composed toward the year 100 A.D.

e. In the last chapter of the last book of the New Testament to be written, it explicitly states that all that Christ said and did was not committed to writing.

2. Another wrong rule of faith is religious liberalism. In general this opinion holds that in religious matters, the intellect should abdicate its superior position in favor of emotion and sentimentality. It holds that feeling is the best guide to truth and the best norm by which to solve a moral problem. Religion should be looked upon as something which soothes and reassures one in time of distress. It is closely linked with the false doctrine of Modernism which was condemned in 1907 by Pius X in the encyclical entitled *Pascendi dominici gregis*. These are its main tenets:

A. Man is autonomous in the field of religion. He must, therefore, reject all external authority that would propose to him a religion binding him to accept definite articles of faith and a code of morals. He condemns them because they are inflexible and rigid.

In answer to this principle we must say briefly that religion is based not on whim or fancy but on the fact that man is dependent on God. Since he cannot escape this dependence, neither can he escape the obligation to practice religion imposed by God.

B. Having proclaimed its autonomy in religious matters, liberalism goes on to state that one should search his heart to discover "truth." In this search one should minimize the role of the intellect and stress the role of the emotions. It further limits the importance of the intellect by saying that it is valid only in the realm of the visible and the sensible.

We shall treat this principle of liberalism more fully in our chapter on the necessity of religion. Suffice it here to state that the obligation to practice religion and the elements of which religion is constituted, make it stable and permanent. The rule of sentimentality attacks the unchanging character of religion for the emotions are neither stable nor permanent. They are variable. By this we mean that although all have the same number of them, their intensity varies at different times and with different persons. They can never be the uniform guide to the truths of religion. No one will deny that the emotions have a place in man's worship of God, for we must worship Him with our whole being. These emotions can be a powerful driving force for good, but liberalism gives them a role which is entirely out of proportion and erroneous.

The powers that make man superior to animal are his intellect and will—his ability to think and to choose. The emotions are blind and indifferent things and therefore inferior to the intellect. They receive their direction from the higher powers and should always be controlled by them. The false rule that we are examining would invert the order of importance of the intellect and will to travel paths dictated by the emotions. Sentiment and emotion is a false rule of faith because it is based on disorder.

C. Religious liberalism gives to the terms *faith, revelation* and *dogma* very peculiar and wrong definitions. By *faith* they do not mean the accepting of a truth on the authority of God Who has revealed it, but rather a special sense by which man unites himself to God. By *revelation* they do not mean the act by which God makes truth known to man but rather the emotional experience by which one feels the nearness of God and this feeling makes one a "believer." By a *dogma* they do not mean a divine truth expressed in set terms, but rather symbols or labels for the different religious emotions which they experience.

There are several other obvious errors inherent in religious liberalism. 1. Truth is immutable. It does not change with times nor persons. It is independent of man's view of it. It is objective and absolute. Liberalism holds that truth varies with persons and times. But both sides of a contradiction cannot be simultaneously true. A thing cannot be and not be at the same time. 2. Liberalism leads to indifference and atheism because of its peculiar theory of knowledge. When it admits the reality of only sensible and visible things, it automatically assumes an agnostic attitude toward the existence of God. We shall see that agnosticism is based on exactly the same principles as atheism.

Utility of Apologetics

1. One need not enter the arena of controversy to discover the usefulness of apologetics. It has great value even for the person who is never asked to defend his faith against opposition. With the help of God's grace, this study can be a powerful auxiliary in helping one to strengthen his faith for it calls explicit attention to the motives for believing. St. Anselm once said, "Fides quaerens intellectum"—the human intellect seeks to understand the doctrines of faith as far as it is able. But some articles of faith are mysteries which we can never fully understand. We must take them on faith. Apologetics shows that our faith in accepting these mysteries is not blind but rather that it is reasonable and fitting and meritorious. It does not involve a debasement of our power of learning nor does it constitute a brake to human progress as some think it does, but it rather elevates the intellect to grasp truths that it could not otherwise discover.

2. A conscientious study of the science of apologetics instills in the mind of the student a deeper love and appreciation for

Holy Mother the Church. It permits one to see her immense strength and influence, the cogency of her credentials, the authority behind her commands, the prudence of her laws, the inerrancy of her teaching. Filial love and devotion to the Church begets a cheerful readiness to obey her in letter and in spirit. It is important that we obey her for she guides us and assists us to attain our primary goal in life, namely, our eternal salvation.

3. A third use of apologetics is that it equips a Catholic to defend his faith. Origen once said that Christ left the task of defending Him to His followers for when He was asked by Pilate to defend Himself He remained silent. Much time and effort has been expended on unstudied defenses of the Church. Many have allowed themselves to be side-tracked into controversies over particular doctrines, such as confession and purgatory, or have tried to explain away certain abuses in the Church such as those at the time of the Renaissance. But this method leaves the basic question unanswered. One should rather fix the discussion on the one fundamental question and reduce multiple inquiries to a single element, namely, church authority. And to discover which church was appointed by God to teach the truths of religion is precisely the task of apologetics. In this matter, the best defense of the Church is a clear explanation of her divine authority. The Catholic Church has its head in heaven but its feet firmly planted on earth and will ever remain a historical fact.

DIVISION OF APOLOGETICS

1. GOD—Five proofs for the existence

In the first section it is proved by reason unaided by revelation that there exists a God, who created man with a spiritual soul. Since the soul has the powers of intellect and will, it follows that man has the obligation to practice religion which is the offering to God the homage of these two powers.

2. CHRIST—Miracles and prophecies

Since Christ's credentials are works attributable only to God, it follows that divine authority vouches for the doctrines which Christ taught and which He intended that all the members of the human race should accept. These doctrines are the articles of supernatural religion.

3. CHURCH—Four Marks

Christ did not choose to remain on earth to teach the articles of supernatural religion, but He founded a teaching agency or church and authorized it to transmit these articles to all men. Christ endowed His Church with four marks of identification by which it could be distinguished from unauthorized churches.

TRUTH ERROR

1. ATHEISM is mistaken because valid proofs

demand that man positively accept God's existence and recognize his dependence on God. Then too, since agnosticism says that man can never learn of God's existence and since indifferentism rejects man's obligation to recognize his dependence on God, these theories are also false.

2. NON-CHRISTIAN religions are mistaken be-

cause even though they accept the existence of God, they reject the valid credentials of Christ—therefore they reject Christ—in support of His divine mission to teach doctrines of faith and morals. The principal non-Christian religions are Mohammedanism, Buddhism, Confucianism, Taoism and Judaism.

3. NON-CATHOLIC sects are mistaken because

even though they accept the existence of God and the credentials of Christ, they nevertheless lack the four marks of identification of the True Church and therefore are not authorized by Christ to teach in His name. The principal non-Catholic sects are the Orthodox, Lutheran, Anglican and some 300 other churches.

II

The Existence of God

THE EXISTENCE of God can be proved by reason without the aid of revelation. In the arguments which are developed here, no mention is made of the Bible or the opinion of any religious leader or the tenets of any church or sect. If these never existed one could still prove that God exists. Man has an intellect or mind, and with this intellect alone he can prove that there is a God.

Man is not born with a clear and precise knowledge of God. God's existence is not self-evident to us as certain principles, such as "The whole is greater than any of its parts," are self-evident. We cannot grasp the knowledge of God's existence in such immediate fashion. If we know that He exists, then a chain of reasoning must precede this conclusion. His existence must be proved and demonstrated. It cannot be presumed.

There are two reasons[1] why we say that God's existence is not self-evident to us. 1. A truth which is self-evident cannot be denied by anyone. But the existence of God is denied by atheists. Therefore it is not self-evident. 2. St. Thomas shows that when a statement is self-evident, the predicate must necessarily be included in the subject. For example, the statement, "The whole is greater than any of its parts," is self-evident because in knowing the meaning of the subject "whole," we immediately see that it includes the predicate "part." To be

1. St. Thomas Aquinas, *Summa Theologica*, Pt. I, Ques. 2, Art. 1.

self-evident the meaning of the terms of these propositions must be known to all. But this cannot be said of our knowledge of God, for all men do not always have a clear notion of the meaning of the term "God." For many, it is confused; for some, it is meaningless. Therefore, the existence of God is not self-evident to us. To possess this knowledge, demonstration is necessary.

There are five basic proofs for the existence of God.[2] It is true that they have certain characteristics in common. Each proof proceeds from an effect to a cause, from the "received" to the "unreceived," but this does not mean that they are five ways of stating a single proof or that one derives added cogency from another. Each is complete in itself.

In each proof for the existence of God, the point of departure is different and therefore the Being whose existence each proof establishes will be seen under a different aspect. This makes for the distinctive character of each of the five "Ways." Notice how the starting points are different. In the world about us we see things as they are moved, as they are caused, as they do not have to exist, as they exhibit limited perfection and as they serve a purpose. With these as starting points we can forge chains of reasoning, the conclusions of which are that there exists a Being Who is the Prime Mover, the First Efficient Cause, the Necessarily Existent, The Source of All Perfection and the Supreme Intelligence. This Being we call God.

Proof from Motion

The first way to prove the existence of God is called the proof from motion. From the fact that there are things in the world which move, it can be shown that there must be a First Mover Who is God. The points of this argument are briefly developed in the following paragraphs.

2. *Ibid.*, Pt. I, Ques. 2, Art. 3.

No one reasonably disputes the fact that there are things which move. One sees a bird in flight, a meteorite hurtling through space, an ocean liner plying its way across the sea. There are hundreds of examples of things moving. Instances of objects moving from place to place are all around us. But in this proof for the existence of God, motion means more than movement from place to place. Carefully notice its meaning here. A thing is said to be in motion when it is gaining or acquiring something which it did not have. Therefore, when a person is acquiring knowledge, he is moving; when he is advancing in age, he is moving; when a plant is growing, it is moving. To further illustrate this, when an acorn is growing into an oak tree, it does not move to another place, but its growth in height and size is an example of a thing in motion. In all the instances listed, the thing was in the process of acquiring a perfection which it did not have and so it was moving.

A thing cannot be in motion and at the same time be at rest. This is impossible. When it begins to move, it is no longer at rest; when it comes to rest, it is no longer in motion. Rest is the absence of motion. But if an object which is now at rest is to acquire motion, from where is it to acquire it? It certainly cannot give this motion to itself, for it does not yet possess it. It can receive motion only from some other object which already has it. A is an object at rest. If A is to move, it must receive motion from B which has it to give to A. A cannot set itself in motion because being at rest, it is devoid of motion. If B, which now gives motion to A, was also at rest at one time, then it received motion from C; C received it from D, and so forth, to the beginning of the series.

Where did motion originally take its rise? It was certainly not derived from any single mover in the series or from all the movers of the series taken together. The reason for this is that the movers taken individually or as a group still have but "received" motion. Extending the series endlessly into the past

does not make it responsible for the motion which is transmitted. "It is necessary to arrive at a first mover which is set
in motion by no other; and this everyone understands to be
God."[3] God then, is a Being outside the series of movers. He
did not receive the power to move from anyone. "He is the
first mover, who acts by Himself, who is his own action and
consequently his own being, for operation follows being, and
the mode of operation the mode of being. The prime mover
. . . must be pure Act . . . and hence, He must be the self-sub-
sisting Being."[4]

Proof from Causality

The starting point of the second proof for the existence of
God is things in the world which are evidently products of an
efficient cause. The statue in the park, the automobile on the
street, the house on the hill, the book on the shelf did not just
happen. They were made.

Not only must we say that this statue was made but we must
also say that it did not make itself. A thing must exist before
it can act. It must itself be before it can produce. It is absurd
to hold that an effect such as a statue or a house existed before
its cause or that an effect is its own cause.

When we are presented with an effect, we must look for its
cause in a being distinct from that effect. In point of time this
cause is the last one which operated. If this last cause was itself
the effect of a previous cause, we shall call that previously existing cause the intermediary cause. In a cause and effect series
there might be a few or there might be many intermediary
causes. But there cannot be so many that the series goes back
endlessly. The impossibility of this lies in the fact that you
cannot have the end of a series without also having a begin-

3. Garrigou-Lagrange, *The One God*, trans. by Dom Bede Rose O.S.B.
(St. Louis; B. Herder Book Co., 1944), p. 141.
    4. *Ibid.*

ning. If one holds that this series of causes and effects goes back endlessly, then he is forced to hold that it never started. And it is as foolish to hold this as it is to hold that there can be a stick with only one end.

Since reason demands that the series of subordinated causes had a beginning, it also demands that this series must have been started by a Being Who owes His power to bring about such an effect to no one. He always possessed this power. He is the First Efficient Cause. And this is but another name for God.

Proof from Contingency

The fact of experience which is the beginning of the third proof for the existence of God is the observation that there are in the world things which exist but which do not have to exist. They are generated and they will corrupt. They are contingent on other things for their existence. Plants and animals clearly belong to this class of things.[5]

There was a time when they did not exist. They exist now; there will come a time when they will pass out of existence.

If the existence of a thing is not necessary—and it is not if it is contingent—then there was a time when it did not exist. Since it clearly cannot attribute its present existence to itself, it must look to a being outside itself as the source of its own existence. The fact that there are things in the world which are dependent upon others points to the existence of a Being Who is not dependent on any other for existence. This Being is God.

If one denies the existence of a necessary being, it is impossible for him to account for the presence of contingent beings in the world. The two are distinct and cannot be confused. Several reasons make it impossible to deny this distinction.

5. Even the laws of nature and the arithmetic tables are contingent; the first would not exist if there was nothing in nature for them to govern; the second on things to be numbered.

1. A great number of dependent beings can never add up to an independent being for the whole cannot be greater than the sum of its parts and many negatives can never add up to a positive.

2. This necessary being is not the material substance of the world which is the substratum of all material contingent things such as plants and animals. The reason for this is that the material world is of a composite character (composed of parts) and is itself dependent on a higher compounding agent for its composition.

3. A necessary being is a perfect being. It is impossible for a perfect being to undergo change. The myriads of changes observable in the world attest to its lack of absolute perfection.

The conclusion to this third proof is this. If one denies the existence of a Necessary Being he must deny the existence of all contingent beings, for they depend on the former. Experience easily proves this to be an absurdity. If, on the other hand, he admits the existence of contingent beings, he must admit the existence of a necessarily existent Being upon whom all depend and who is called God.

We do well, here, to notice the difference between the proofs for the existence of God from causality and from contingency. They are not the same. In the proof from causality we look at things as they are products of an efficient cause and eventually conclude to the existence of a First Efficient Cause. In the proof from contingency we look at things under the aspect of objects which do not have to exist and eventually conclude to the existence of a Being Who must necessarily exist. The two proofs are quite different from each other.

Degrees of Perfection

In the world about us we see things that possess perfection. We see things that are good, true, beautiful, living and the like. These perfections are *in themselves* limitless or inex-

haustible but the things that possess them have them in vary-
ing degrees and in a limited fashion. For example, an animal
has a higher degree of life than does a plant; a human has a
higher degree of life than does an animal. The same could be
said of the other perfections.

When we look at the life that this particular thing, e.g. tree,
possesses it is quite evident that it does not possess the perfection of life in its entirety for there are many other living things
in existence. In fact, the tree possesses life in an extremely
limited degree. Now if we combined all the living things in
the world, this aggregate would still not exhaust this perfection. No matter how great or how many living things of limited perfection could be combined they still would not constitute all *possible* life for the term "life" of itself does not
admit of any limitation.

Since this tree has a limited degree of the perfection of life,
it clearly cannot be the source of all this perfection nor can
it even be the source of its own perfection. In fact it makes
no difference how great a limited thing is, it cannot possess
an exhaustless perfection for the finite cannot contain the infinite. It follows then that a limited perfection is a received
perfection. And if there are things in existence possessing limited or received perfections, as indeed there are, there must
exist a Being Who possesses perfection in an inexhaustible and
infinite degree. This Being we call God.

Proof from Design

The starting point for the fifth proof for the existence of
God is the observation that there are about us things which
serve a purpose. The cogency of this argument is not weakened because of the fact that the purposefulness of many objects cannot readily be named. If there were but one instance
of usefulness in the whole universe, this proof would be still
valid.

There are many things in the world which were made for a definite reason. Man has eyes to see and ears to hear; birds have wings to fly; fishes have gills to breathe; an eagle has talons to grasp. Many other instances of purposefulness could be given. In each object the parts were fitted together in such a manner that a definite goal might be attained. A different arrangement of the same parts would not bring about the same result. The parts of the eye are so arranged that sight may be had; wings are so made up that they may sustain the bird in flight; a root is designed to play an integral part in the life of the plant.

The designing of a useful thing involves several factors. It takes intelligence to arrange the parts of an object so that it will serve a purpose. The designer must first conceive his goal. Then he must know how the parts are to be arranged so that this goal will be reached. These two steps must be thought out abstractly before the work of fitting the parts together can begin. But abstract thought requires an immaterial thinking power called intelligence. Material things, because they are material, are not capable of abstract thought.

An object such as an eye or an ear is purposeful, yet is wholly material. It does not have the power to think or plan. It, therefore, could not have designed itself. An outside intelligence must have been in operation in designing the eye. The eye which exhibits purposefulness we shall call A. Being material, it clearly did not design itself. The designing intelligence we shall call B. If B is a limited intelligence, then it was given intelligence by C. The existence of a series of beings in which each intelligence received its intelligence from another intelligent being does not account for the source of all intelligence. One must ultimately admit the existence of a being whose intelligence was not acquired from another. This being is called the "Unacquired Intelligence." This is but another name for God. Therefore, God exists.

Having proved the existence of God we now move on to

investigate His nature, using our intellects unaided by revelation as our only instrument.

Nature of God

Even though we cannot comprehend the nature of God, we can learn something about it by the use of reason.

One way of learning the nature of an object is to notice how it acts. Everything must act according to its nature or mode of existence. A stone must act like a stone; a plant like a plant and an animal like an animal. A stone cannot act like a plant, for it clearly cannot exercise powers that it does not have. It can only exercise powers that it does have. The proofs for the existence of God have shown us how God has acted and from this we learn something of His nature.

It is well here to fix the meaning of the terms nature (essence) and existence. The essence of a thing is that which makes a thing what it is. It sets it apart from other things. It gives it its distinctive character. Existence is that which lifts a thing out of the realm of possibility and places it in the realm of actuality and we saw above that there is no creature in the latter which was not once in the former.

Science tells us that because of atmospheric conditions, there was a time when no man existed on earth. At that time, the nature of man existed but existed only in the realm of possibility. From this it is easy to see that there is nothing about human nature or any other created nature which demands that it must have actual existence. Science is attempting to determine when man first appeared on the face of the earth. It is trying to fix the time when this human nature which had previously existed only in the realm of possibility was combined with the perfection called actual existence. Looking at a creature from this point of view is important. It shows that man is a combination of essence and existence. Essence remained only possible until it was lifted into the status of an actual being by the advent of existence. Every creature is a compound of these two elements.

Every compound presupposes the pre-existence of a compounding agent that brought it about. In the proofs for the existence of God we saw that nothing which is merely possible can make itself actual by annexing to itself the perfection of existence. This combination can only be effected by an external agent.

All of the five proofs for God's existence brought out the point that there was absolutely nothing prior to God in existence. For this reason we must say that there was no power that could make in God a combination of any kind. God has an essence and an existence but they are not found in combination. They are one and the same. It is His nature to exist. Man is a nature with existence. But God's essence or nature is existence. "Thus the supreme truth of philosophy or the fundamental truth of judgment is that in God alone essence and existence are identified."[6]

Several conclusions flow from the fact that God's essence is identical with His Existence.

1. *He is a Spirit*—God must be a spirit because He is devoid of all composition. Indeed we proved that there is no being prior to God who could effect a composition. He is not material for material objects have measurable parts and these presuppose composition. The human soul is a spirit because it too does not have measurable parts but it is still a composite of essence and existence. Since God has neither parts nor composition, He is a perfectly simple spirit.

2. *He is infinitely perfect*—In the fourth proof for the existence of God, it was pointed out that being is a perfection which of itself does not imply limitation of any kind. Things in the world about us have limited being or perfection because they have limited existence. Limitation must be imposed by a limiting cause. Since there is no being prior to God that

6. Garrigou-Lagrange, *op. cit.,* p. 153.

could in any way limit Him, we must conclude that He is an infinite being. To be infinite being is to be infinite perfection for perfection cannot exist without being.

3. *He is immutable*—By divine immutability we mean that God can in no way change. This flows from the fact that He is infinitely perfect. Change of any kind implies imperfection. When a thing gains by change, it implies imperfection in the past. When it loses by change, it implies imperfection in the present. God does neither. He cannot gain because He is already infinitely perfect. He cannot lose part of His being because He does not possess parts. For God to lose anything He would have to lose everything. He would have to be completely destroyed, but this is absolutely impossible. His nature is to exist. God is, then, immutable.

4. *He is necessarily eternal*—Eternity is infinity under the aspect of duration. As has been repeatedly pointed out God exists but He owes His existence to no one. He does not have a "received" existence and so He never had a beginning. Since He is in no way changeable, He cannot have an end. These are the notes of a necessarily eternal Being and God alone has them.

In attempting to grasp the meaning of God's eternity we must carefully avoid thinking that He existed and will exist for an endless number of centuries. 1—"An endless series" is a contradiction. A series cannot be endless. It must have a beginning and end for otherwise it is not a series. 2—A series implies succession and succession implies change. God has neither; with God there is no such thing as past and future. There is only the present.

5. *He is unique*—When we say that God is unique we mean that not only is He one but there can be none other equal to Him. When we say that God is infinitely perfect, we mean that He possesses all *possible* perfection. There is no perfection actual or possible that God does not already possess. If there could be two Gods, then it is a manifest contradiction

to say that they both possessed all possible perfection. One would be limited by what the other had and so neither could be infinite. Since God is infinite, He is unique.

6. *He is Omnipotent*—God can do all things. He can bring into the realm of actuality anything that is in the realm of possibility. There is no effect that He cannot produce. Since effects of their very nature are finite, it follows that no number of effects can exhaust the infinite power or perfection of God and so He is omnipotent.

7. *He is Omniscient*—He knows all things past, present, future, and possible. We proved that God is the Supreme Intelligence. There is no perfection that He does not already possess. It follows then, that God in knowing Himself knows all that has, will and can come to pass and so He is omniscient.

8. *He is Omnipresent*—God is everywhere. This follows from the fact that He is an infinitely perfect spirit. Not only is He everywhere but He is everywhere in His entirety for being a spirit He is not composed of parts that would confine one to a single place.

Atheism

It is proper that we conclude this chapter with a few remarks about the fallacies which either deny the existence of God or propound confused notions about His nature. These errors are atheism, agnosticism, and pantheism. Agnosticism and pantheism are but refinements of atheism because they attack the same principles that atheism attacks.

Atheism is the error which holds that no personal God exists. A person is a being with an intellect and will. In place of a being with power and knowledge, this fallacy substitutes a blind cosmic force or its equivalent.

Agnosticism does not unconditionally deny the existence of God. But it does deny that man can prove His existence. It protests that since man's capacity for learning is limited, he can never grasp the existence of a being whose perfection is unlimited. It fails to see that one can know the existence of a thing without knowing it exhaustively. Man can know the existence of God because the object of his intellect is not merely finite being but being in general.

Pantheism denies the existence of a supreme being who is distinct from the material universe. As the name implies, this error holds that the conglomerate of all existing things is God regardless of their mode of existence.

Those who deny the existence of God as we have proved, admit that if the principles on which the five proofs are based are allowed to stand, then the conclusions drawn from them will be valid. They, therefore, attack the validity of these principles. These are the fundamental principles used to prove God's existence. 1. The principle of identity is that a thing must be itself. 2. The principle of contradiction says that a thing cannot be and not be at the same time. 3. The principle of causality is that every effect must have a cause. These principles do not apply only to material things but to all being whether it be material or non-material.

The principles of identity and contradiction are self-evident and cannot be denied without denying the existence of all being . . . a conclusion to which atheists by their activity show that they do not subscribe. When atheists attack the principle of causality they equivalently attack the principle of contradiction for they are forced to hold that a thing can at once be moved and non-moved, caused and non-caused, contingent and non-contingent. It is easy to see that a denial of the validity of the principles of identity, contradiction, and causality leads to absurdity. Since these principles are valid, so are the proofs for the existence of God and the systems of atheism, agnosticism and pantheism must be labeled fallacious.

The greatest number of atheists are not theoretical atheists but rather practical atheists. We have seen that it is impossible to have a valid chain of arguments disproving the existence of

God. But even though they cannot disprove the existence of God, there is nothing to prevent some people from living as though there is no God. And those who live as though there is no God are called practical atheists.

The most fruitful source of practical atheism is immorality. All men seek happiness and peace of mind. They know that to have a lively consciousness of the existence and sanction of God and at the same time to continue to live immorally is disquieting and frustrating. They must make a choice. They choose the immorality and proceed to attempt to crush out of their lives a disturbing consciousness of God until they, in practice, live as though He did not exist. They have then become practical atheists.

III

The Existence of the Soul

An important link in the chain of inquiries which make up the science of apologetics is the existence in man of a spiritual soul. The errors which apologetics must refute are not merely errors from history. They are also errors from philosophy. In fact the impact of the emphasis on material science has given rise to an increasing number of philosophical errors in recent decades. One such popular error has been that known as positivism or materialism, which holds that nothing exists but matter or that which is perceptible to the senses. If a person could be persuaded to accept this falsehood he would implicitly be forced to deny the freedom of the will and existence of a life hereafter. Concomitantly, the obligation to practice religion would be stripped of its cogency. It would be an empty shell. Materialists are entirely conscious of this. We must show that to deny the existence of the soul is to run counter to reason and common sense.

Men in general believe that each human person has an immortal soul. But there are many, holding to a materialistic view of things, who flatly deny the soul's existence. They cannot *see* the soul; therefore, they argue, it does not exist. These materialists do not admit the possibility of revelation for the soul's existence. They must be met, then, on rational grounds; we must establish from reason alone that man does have a soul.

Man has often been compared with animals. Certain species of animals have a bodily structure so similar to man's that some have denied that there is any real difference between the two. They say that man is but a high-type animal. But in making a comparison, one should note the points not only of similarity, but also of dissimilarity. The key to any correct comparison lies in showing how two things are not the same. The difference between man and animals is that, although they are very similar in bodily structure, man has a spiritual soul, whereas animals have not.

In listing the difference between two things, writers have often called attention to the fact that one could do something which the other could not do. What was possible for one was impossible for the other. This is a clear-cut way of pointing out differences, for it indicates the presence of a power or perfection in one, and its absence in the other, thereby showing that they are not identically the same.

Intellect

Man is able to think. Several things are involved in the conception of a thought or idea. In the first place, man must perceive something in the world about him. He must first perceive and form an image of something. He sees a plant, an animal, a building, a chair and so forth. But the image he perceives—for example, an auto—fits only one particular car of definite color, make and model. It does not fit all cars because it has characteristics or notes which other cars do not have. It is of singular application.

When an image of an auto has been formed, man has a power called the intellect which strips away from the image of "this" car all the notes which belong only to it. It removes the individualizing characteristics of this image or picture. The intellect loses sight of those things which make this car different from that car. It does not conceive of a car being of this particular color or make. It simply grasps what all cars must have to be called cars. The object which the intellect conceives after stripping away the individualizing notes of an image is called a *concept* or an idea. This idea of an auto fits all autos of the past, present, and future. It is universally applicable to that class of things known as cars. And because an idea is universally applicable it is immaterial; it is not made up of parts; it cannot be seen or touched. Material things can be seen and touched because they are singular; representations of them are applicable to only one definite object.

Since an idea is immaterial it must be conceived by a power which is of the same order, that is to say, the intellect is an immaterial power. Being immaterial or devoid of parts, the intellect operates independently of the body. After it has been set in motion by the perception of a sensible thing such as a plant or animal, it does not need the brain in order to conceive an abstract idea of this thing.

There is another solid reason for saying that man's intellect is an immaterial power. It is the fact that it can reflect upon its own operations. It can turn its attention upon itself and analyze its own activities. Reflection is impossible for a material organ, that is, for a faculty which is made up of parts. The eye is material and so cannot see itself seeing; the ear cannot hear itself hearing. But the intellect can know itself thinking thus proving that it is an immaterial power. Other indications of the intellect being an immaterial power are man's ability to speak and to progress, that is, to improve upon his own inventions. These activities involve the ability to form abstract ideas and to appreciate the relations between them after they are once formed.

What is the object of the intellect? What does it know? The intellect does not merely grasp things as they are colored or resonant or savory. It does not merely consider the externals of a thing. It lays hold of the nature of an object. But for man to know a thing, that thing must have some sort of existence. If it exists, it has some kind of being. Man cannot form an idea of nothingness. A thing which exists need not be material; it can be immaterial. Since man can directly or indirectly come to know all things, created and uncreated, finite and infinite, actual and possible, material and spiritual, the object of the intellect is being in general.

Will

Experience plainly shows that man has the ability to strive to possess things which he knows. The guide to his striving power is his knowing power for he must know a thing before he can exert himself to possess it. Man's striving power is called his will.

Like the intellect, the will is an immaterial power. It can strive to possess anything which is presented to it as good or desirable. These goods need not be of the material order. They can be immaterial as well. Man can strive to possess such immaterial goods as justice and honor; he can exert himself to master an abstract science. Since the will can strive to possess any type of good, it must be an immaterial power. A material organ can only strive to possess a material thing.

In its action the will is free. It is at liberty to choose one of several courses of action or one of several things; it can choose not to make a choice. There is no force which can compel the will to act in a certain way.

An outside force cannot compel the will to act in a determined way or even to act at all. It can only bring its influence to bear on acts which flow from the will. For example, walking may be physically imposed on him by an outside force but his will does not give consent. External compulsion cannot reach the will. However because of compulsion man can be induced to consent to a course of action which his will would not otherwise embrace.

There is nothing internal to the will which forces it to make this or that choice. The key argument in showing that the will is internally free lies in the fact that the intellect which guides the will cannot be forced to judge a particular good to be desirable in every respect. The will is a blind power. It can only strive to possess that which the intellect presents to it as good or desirable. If the intellect knows a thing to be universally good and perfectly desirable, it must judge it as such, and then the will must choose it. But if a thing is partially desirable and partially undesirable—as is the case with all earthly things —there is nothing about it which obliges the intellect to judge it as wholly desirable. The intellect can concentrate on the imperfect features of a given thing and then judge it as undesirable. Since the intellect is not obliged to judge the value of a partially good thing in a determined way, it can freely change its estimate of it. And because the intellect is free in changing its judgment, the will is free in its choice for the intellect guides the will. Instead of being forced to act in a certain way, it is the will which determines which of several judgments on a certain subject shall be the last one and the one to be acted upon.

Another argument for the freedom of the will is the fact that it is the universal opinion of men that they are responsible for their actions. There has never been a nation on the face of the earth which did not have rules to keep order and machinery to administer justice. These things would be meaningless if man were not free. It would be impossible to explain these and similar phenomena if man were forced or determined to act in a definite way.

Soul

A man's intellect and will are powers of a single immaterial substance called the human soul.

A soul is an immaterial substance. By substance is meant something which can exist by itself. It does not have to exist in something else. Color, for example, is not a substance. We never see color existing by itself. We always see things which are colored. The thing in which color inheres exists by itself. It is a substance. Noticing carefully what substance means, one can see that a substance need not be material, it need not have parts. If it exists by itself, it is a substance. The human soul is a substance which does not have parts. It is immaterial because it must be of the same order as its powers, namely the intellect and will which are immaterial powers. The soul, then, does not need the body to exist.

Each member of the human race has but one soul or spirit. A man is conscious of acting as a unity. He does not say, "My intellect thinks," or, "My will desires." Rather, he says, "I think and I desire." But another reason for saying that man has but one soul is that it would be difficult, if not impossible, for intellect and will to function if they inhered in separate substances. They influence each other. The will must have a desirable thing presented to it by the intellect before it can strive to possess it. The intellect is driven to enrich its store of knowledge by the will. Now if the intellect and will were powers of separate substances they could not exert their influence on each other. But since they do act, they must be powers of one spiritual substance called the soul.

Corollary I

When is a thing dead? A thing dies or corrupts when it dissolves into its component parts. An eye is destroyed when its parts are so deranged by an injury or disease that it can no longer carry on the function of sight. The same is true of the other organs of man. Expanding this somewhat, it is clear that when a living thing breaks down into its component parts so that it can no longer carry on the function of life it is dead. But notice carefully what death implies. It implies that the living thing must have parts which are able to dissociate or dissolve. Only material things have parts. The soul of man, however, has no parts. The soul, therefore, cannot die. It is immortal. It can only pass out of existence by annihilation, that is, if God would withdraw from the soul His sustaining might which preserves it in existence. But it is indestructible by natural means.

Corollary II

What type of cause is required to produce a soul? It is clearly impossible for the soul to be produced by a material cause for then the immaterial would have sprung from the material, the immortal from the mortal and dissoluble; an effect would be produced which is greater than the cause.

It is impossible for the soul to have a "parent" soul which is limited and finite. The souls of men, angels and devils are finite spirits but they cannot bring other souls or spirits into existence. They cannot create a soul for this requires unlimited power. They cannot produce a soul by dividing themselves in the manner of reproduction of the lower plants and animals because this process cannot be carried out with a thing which does not have parts.

There remains but one way in which the soul can be produced. It is creation. Creation is an action proper to a Being Who has unlimited power. This Infinite Cause is God and He it is Who directly creates every human soul which is infused into a body.

IV

The Necessity of Religion

ONE OF THE MOST striking features of recorded history is the fact that there never was a race of people which did not have some notion of religion. The archeological discoveries in Egypt and in the Middle East have never failed to produce fresh evidence of the part that it played in the lives of the people who lived several millenia before Christ. It is true that most of the evidence shows that the people were polytheists. But the important thing is that they recognized the existence of a being to whom homage was due. In the pagan Roman world the duties of civil officials were partially of a religious nature. Even today in the technologically backward countries of the world the people recognize their obligation to practice religion.

A phenomenon as widespread and as enduring as the practice of religion cannot be ascribed to custom or arbitrary legislation. Its roots must be deeper. Custom and legislation have been radically different in different ages and among different peoples. But the main features of religion have been perfectly stereotyped among all the nations of history. It is important to discover the precise meaning of religion and to seek the basis for its stability.

Religion Taken Objectively

Every goal requires the proper means to attain it. We will see that God is man's supreme goal in life. It is indeed in accordance with right reason to hold that definite means must be employed to reach this end. These means are embodied in the definition of religion taken objectively. As it is in itself, *religion* is defined as *the sum of truths and precepts whereby one's life is directed to God.* It will not do to say that haphazard and arbitrary means will be successful in this important endeavor any more than it would be reasonable to hold that a sea captain would reach his destination if he entirely disregarded his chart and instruments.

How is man going to learn the doctrines that will guide him to his goal? He is certainly not born with them for if this were the case, all men would have the same views on this subject. They patently do not. The truths of religion are not innate. They must be acquired. And there are two ways by which he can learn them. He can either discover them by the use of reason or he can have them revealed to him by God.

1. *Natural religion is the name given to the complexus of truths and precepts which man can discover by the natural light of reason.* Reason, alone, for example, can arrive at the fact that there exists but one Supreme Being upon Whom all are dependent, that man has an immortal soul; that he has certain duties to God, to his neighbor and to himself which are the precepts of the natural law.

We say that unaided reason can discover the truths of natural religion but we must hasten to add that this is by no means an easy task. It requires continued intellectual application and leisure in which to pursue the inquiries. Most people have neither. For the majority of men, the pressing task of making a living seems to be of paramount importance and so they devote their time and ability to what to them seems most important. Projects which do not bring speedy and tangible results do not arrest their attention. It must be said that if the generality of men are left to their own devices they will not acquire the truths of natural religion even though they have the equipment to do so.[1]

1. St. Thomas Aquinas, *Contra Gentiles.*

Perhaps the rank and file of men could learn the articles of natural religion from the philosophers—the men who had the time and ability to engage in prolonged intellectual labors? But a study of pagan Greek and Latin philosophy shows that the thinkers themselves did not have clear notions on this subject. To say the least, they were a very confused lot. Protagoras, Gorgias of Leontine, Pyrrho, and many others said that philosophical investigation was futile for there is no valid knowledge. Democritus and Leucippus denied the existence of a spiritual, immortal soul. Heraclitus, Parmenides and the Stoics identified God with the material universe and the Academicians held contradictory opinions concerning his nature [2] Plato would arbitrarily impose on all the religion of the fatherland which was mainly polytheism.[3] Socrates said that knowledge is virtue and ignorance is vice, while the Epicureans said that a thing is morally good if it is pleasurable. The philosophers before the time of Anaxagoras were characterized as "a group of random talkers"[4] and Cicero said that no matter how wild an opinion might be, there could be found men who held it.[5] The thinkers not only lacked authority to have their conclusions accepted but in some instances their efforts were repaid with ingratitude. Socrates was forced to commit suicide by drinking the hemlock and Aristotle had to flee the Athenians "so as not to give them an opportunity of offending a second time against philosophy."

The fruitlessness of the efforts of pre-Christian thinkers in discovering the doctrines of natural religion was neatly captured in a saying ascribed to Plato—probably falsely so—which reads, "We must wait until someone comes to show us how to conduct ourselves towards the gods and towards our fellowmen." The history of pagan thought in all ages delivers one

2. Cicero, De Natura Deorum I. 1.
3. Republic I. 4.
4. Aristotle, Metaphysics I. 3. 984b.
5. De Divinatione 58.

of the most crushing arguments against that tenet of rationalism which holds that man never need be given outside assistance in discovering the truths that will guide him to his goal in life.

2. Although we can say that revelation by God is morally necessary if all men are to learn the truths of religion quickly and infallibly, we cannot conclude that it has already taken place. It is clearly illogical to say that a thing exists because it is fitting that it should exist. In historical matters, there is no substitute for investigation and evidence.

Even before the inquiry into the actuality of revelation begins, rationalists say that it has not taken place because it is impossible. They rightly conclude that if a thing is impossible, to inquire into its existence is wasted effort. But the weakness of the rationalist position lies in the fact that they cannot prove how the making of a revelation involves a contradiction that would render it impossible.

If the revelation of the articles of supernatural revelation could not take place, then the impediment would arise from one of the elements involved, that is God or man or the doctrines revealed. But none of these presents a difficulty. In the first place, God being infinite in power and knowledge does not lack the ability to make truths known to men; nor is He powerless in providing criteria whereby we will know with certainty that the doctrines are from Him. Next, revelation is not impossible because man can receive it, for if he can be taught by other men, he certainly can be taught by God. Finally, one does not have to know a revealed truth exhaustively or comprehensively before he can know that it exists, as is the case even in the natural order. In the light of these considerations we are warranted in saying that divine revelation is possible.

If it can be proved that supernatural revelation is a historical fact, then man is not free to practice natural religion. God might require more of us than what is contained in natural religion. "The unaided light of reason can attain only a mediate knowledge of God by means of the study of His creatures and must consequently be imperfect. The study of nature can result only in the knowledge of such truths as are necessarily connected with it, and can tell us nothing about any free acts which God may have performed above and beyond nature, the knowledge of which He may nevertheless require of us."[6]

Religion Taken Subjectively

As it applies to us, religion is defined as: *Man's recognition of the existence of God, and the worship of Him because of His excellence and sovereignty over all things.* It may be described as the virtue that man practices when he makes God the goal of his life. There are several ways to prove that the practice of religion is not merely an optional matter as the indifferentists say but rather it is of strict obligation.

I. It was proved that man like all creatures is a being dependent on God for his existence, perfection and preservation. Everything he has, he has received. But unlike inanimate and irrational beings he has the power to recognize this dependence.

When man gives practical expression to this act of recognizing his dependence on a Higher Being, he practices religion. Since the dependence of man on God is absolute and unescapable, then the obligation to recognize it and to act accordingly is also absolute and unescapable. It is incumbent on all who have an intellect and free will and not only on those who wish to accept it. Its basis is not in the realm of sentiment or temperament or choice. It is rooted in man's contingent nature.

There are three elements in the act of religion. They are adoration, thanksgiving and love. Adoration is the very act of recognizing one's dependence on God. It can be explicit or

6. Wilhelm-Scannell, *Manual of Catholic Theology* (London; Kegan-Paul, Trench, Trubner and Co. Ltd., 1890), I, 6.

implicit. It is explicit when the mind focuses its attention upon it and acknowledges the dependence in set terms or actions. It is implicit when it is made by performing an act (e.g. prayer) which presupposes the recognition. It is clear that thanksgiving and love flow naturally from adoration.

II. A second argument for the necessity of religion is based on man's desire to be happy. This craving is not found in isolated instances among men nor does it vary from country to country. It is constant and universal among the members of the human race. They are born with it and never outgrow it.

The things of this world can only produce imperfect happiness. If they satisfy a person in one respect they will fail to do so in another. But even if they could satisfy one in every respect so that there was nothing else that he could desire, they still would be imperfect for they must end with death. Wealth, power and pleasure are clearly imperfect goods. They cannot completely fill up man's craving for happiness. The wealth of the Gracchi was imperfect for there was much wealth elsewhere which they did not possess. There were many things it could not buy. The great power of an Alexander did not save him from the despair of not having new worlds to conquer. The Epicureans realized that their pleasures would be abruptly ended for they said, "Let us eat, drink and be merry for tomorrow we die." These goods are essentially imperfect and a string of imperfect goods can never add up to a perfect one.

Man seeks perfect happiness. He consciously and unconsciously strives to have complete satisfaction for an unending period—a satisfaction that will not end in death. Perfect happiness can be produced only by the possession of a perfect good. The tasting of the imperfect only intensifies the desire for the perfect.

Somewhere there must exist a good that can make man perfectly happy. God does nothing in vain for He is infinite wisdom. Everything He does has a meaning and a purpose. With this in mind, it would be against God's wisdom for Him to implant in every man the desire to be perfectly happy without there being anything that could fill up this desire. It is absurd to hold that He has acted in vain by giving man a craving which must forever remain frustrated. We must conclude that there exists a good that can make man perfectly happy.

God is the only perfect Being or Good for He alone is infinite in every respect. By possessing God we become perfectly happy. This possession produces a complete ecstasy which never ends. St. Augustine beautifully summarized God's role in our lives and happiness when, speaking to God, he said, "For Thyself, Thou hast created us, O God, and our hearts are not at rest until they rest in Thee."[7]

A study of man's manner of acting proves that if he wishes to possess the happiness that his nature craves, he must make God the goal of his life. Now this is but another way of saying that his nature demands that he practice religion. Since the desire to be perfectly happy is unescapable, the obligation to practice religion is also unescapable.

III. The third proof for the necessity of religion flows from the fact that God is the supreme and primary object of man's intellect and will. We have seen that it is the possession of these two powers that separates man from the animal world. We shall now see what he must do to most ennoble them.

Man has an intellect with which he is able to think abstractly. He is able to conceive ideas, judge, and reason. His intellect has a definite object just as his other powers have theirs. For example, the object of sight is things as they reflect light or color; that of hearing is things as they are resonant, while that of taste is things as they are savory, and so forth. The object of the intellect is to know things as they are. It is to grasp their nature, to form ideas which correctly embody the essence of an article. When a person knows things as they actually are, he is said to possess logical truth.

Some truths are worthier of note than others. There is a

7. *Confessions* Bk. I. 1.

definite gradation of values among the things that we can know. It is better to know a theorem of geometry than the answer to some simple mathematical problem. It is more profitable to grasp a principle of philosophy than the magnitude of a distant star. It is of greater value to know the properties of chemical elements than the composition of some stone that a workman fits into the wall. All of these are examples of truth yet some are clearly more worth knowing than others. But man should by all means strive to know the higher and the more perfect truths for in knowing them the intellect is evidently put to a better use.

The supreme truth that man can know is that God exists. He is an infinite being and so there is not, nor can there be, anything worthier of note. It is plain that man puts his intellect to the best possible use when he uses it to know God. And since there can be no substitute for God in the order of importance, it follows that to know Him is the primary reason why this power was given to us.

Paralleling man's use of his intellect is the use of his will. The object of man's will is things which are presented to him as good or desirable. And like truth, they are on different levels of worth and importance. Intellectual values are better than material goods; the permanent is better than the momentary; the universal better than the particular and so on. Although all are good, some are more valuable than others. But man should aim to possess the highest good, for the higher the good the will possesses the more is it ennobled, for it is put to better use.

The supreme Good that man can strive to possess is God for He is Infinite Goodness. All the good there is in creation is but a shadow of the Being Who is the source of all perfection. Man puts his will to its best possible use when he uses it to possess God. This is the primary reason why this power was given to him.

Since the primary reason why man was given an intellect

and will is to know and to possess God, it follows that his primary duty in life is to practice religion. In using his highest powers properly man makes God the goal of his life. Since the goal cannot be replaced, the obligation to seek it cannot be escaped.

In summary we say that man's obligation to practice religion stems from the fact that he is absolutely dependent on God for his whole being, that he cannot escape the desire to be perfectly happy, and that the supreme object of his intellect and will is unlimited truth and goodness.

Although all are bound by the obligation to practice religion, it does not mean that all will fulfill it. Man has it within his power to ignore the obligations which his nature shows to be right and just. He has often deceived himself by exchanging the goal of perfect happiness for transient pleasures. At times, he has perverted the primary use of his intellect and will by crushing God out of his life and then attempting to replace Him with some secondary truth or good.

If it can be proved that God has revealed to man how He is to be worshipped, then man must obey Him to the letter. He is left no choice in the matter. God, being the Superior, would be entirely within His rights to lay down the articles of faith and precepts of morals which man must accept.

The question of whether or not God has made supernatural revelation to man leads one to investigate the soundness of the foundations of the different religions in existence today. They claim to be the agencies through which God transmits to man the articles of revelation. The procedure that will be followed in this book will be to investigate the foundations of Christianity for evidence of divine authority and revelation. If Christianity is found wanting, then one would be warranted to investigate the non-Christian religions. If all are found wanting, then man must live according to the tenets of natural religion.

If we examine the works of Christian apologists of all ages, we find that they appeal extensively to the Old and New Testaments to prove their points. They make special use of the Gospels. The use of the Gospels is not the only means that Christian writers use to defend their position, but it must be admitted that their use greatly facilitates the inquiry. They can be looked upon as the apologetical source of Christianity. But before the Gospels can be used in connection with apologetics, their worth and reliability must be proved. To do this we must examine them from the points of view of integrity, authorship, and historicity.

In any discussion on the historical value of the Gospels, the doctrine of inspiration must be safeguarded. As writings inspired by God, the Gospels are perfectly trustworthy. It is the purpose of the next three chapters to show that we need not appeal to inspiration to prove their reliability. This can be done by applying to them the criteria which are used to test the historical worth of even profane documents.

Part Two

THE EXISTENCE OF REVELATION

V

The Integrity of the Gospels

THE TEXT of a writing is integral if no additions or subtractions were made to it throughout the period of its existence. An investigation into the integrity of the Gospels, then, entails, the tracing of the condition of the text down through the ages. If it can be proved that it is the same today as it was when it was originally written, then it is integral.

The Gospels are part of that group of writings known as the New Testament. These writings, with the exception of the First Gospel,[1] were originally written in Koine or colloquial Greek. None of the autographs of these compositions are extant today, but there have been catalogued some 4,280 very old manuscripts[2] or fragments of manuscripts of the New Testament. This fact is important because it shows how well supported the modern critical editions are which are made from a comparison or collation of these manuscripts. Not one of the ancient Latin or Greek classics is supported by as much manuscript evidence as is the New Testament.[3]

In examining the mass of Greek New Testament manu-

1. Papias in Eusebius, H.E. III. xxxix. 16.
2. Photostats of many of them are reproduced in W.H.P. Hatch's work, *The Principal Uncial Manuscripts of the New Testament* (University of Chicago Press, 1939).
3. Robertson, *Textual Criticism of the New Testament* (London; Hodder & Staughton Ltd., 1925), pp. 70ff; Kenyon, *Our Bible and the Ancient Manuscripts* (New York; Harper & Bros., 1941), pp. 98ff.

scripts, scholars have noted certain characteristics about these manuscripts which permit the whole mass to be broken down into four main families. However, a listing of these characteristics would not appreciably further the inquiry in a summary discussion such as this. They are adequately considered in any text book on the introduction to the New Testament.[4] But the existence of these characteristics is useful because it permits scholars to fix the date of these families of manuscripts since the families appear in the works of ancient authors whose dates are well known.

When the four families of manuscripts are compared with each other, it is noticed that the readings are essentially the same. Remembering the fact that the modern critical editions are made from a collation of these manuscripts,[5] one can conclude that the modern text of the New Testament goes back to the time of the oldest of these families or to at least 200 A.D.

The text of the Gospels in its present condition can be traced to a period prior to 200 A.D. in the following manner. From about 175 A.D. to about 215 A.D. there flourished in Europe, North Africa and Asia Minor ecclesiastical writers who wrote many treatises on theological and apologetical subjects. The most important of these writers were St. Irenaeus of Lyons in Gaul (c. 130/140–203), Clement of Alexandria in Egypt (c. 150–211) and Tertullian of Carthage in North Africa (c. 150/160–220). Many of their writings are extant today and they abound in literally thousands of quotations from the Bible. An actual count shows that St. Irenaeus quotes the New Testament 1819 times, Clement of Alexandria quotes it

4. Steinmueller, *A Companion to Scripture Studies* (New York; J. F. Wagner, Inc., 1941), pp. 150ff.

5. It is possible that there are some important Gospel manuscripts still undiscovered. In 1951, Dr. Aziz Suryal Atiya of Farouk University in Cairo found a very old five-layer palimpsest of the Gospels while microfilming ancient writings in the Monastery of St. Catherine on Mt. Sinai. It will be known henceforth as MS, Arabicus but it will be some time before its real value can be determined.

2406 times and Tertullian quotes it the incredible number of 7259 times. So frequently, in fact, does Tertullian quote the New Testament that a German scholar by the name of Ronsch was able to reproduce most of it from the works of this African writer alone. The same could be done from the works of the other two writers. Now if a composite were made of the New Testament quotations found in the works of these writers and that composite were compared to the New Testament as it is today, one would discover that the readings are essentially the same. This shows that the modern text of the New Testament was in existence in the second half of the Second Century.

In the Second Century there lived a writer named Tatian (c. 120–180) who composed a "Diatesseron" or Harmony of the Gospels. In this work, Tatian used all the Gospels to compose, probably in Syriac, one continuous narrative of the Gospels. For a long time the "Diatesseron" was lost until its Arabic translation was found and edited by Ciasca in 1888. This discovery is important because it shows that the text of the Gospels of modern times is essentially the same as the one which lay before Tatian when he wrote his "Diatesseron" shortly after the middle of the Second Century. But since Tatian became acquainted with the Gospels through Justin the Martyr, who converted him, the text of the Gospels goes back to the time of St. Justin Martyr, or to about 140 A.D.

It takes time for essential changes to creep into the text of a writing. The Gospels existed in essentially their present textual condition in about 140 A.D. The best scholars assign the composition of the first of the Gospels to about from 60 A.D. to 75 A.D. Now the period of time which intervenes between 75 A.D. to 140 A.D. is too short to allow essential corruptions to creep into the text. This statement can be supported by the authority of Von Soden[6] whose opinion is very weighty in matters of New Testament textual criticism.

The statement of Von Soden concerning the integrity of

6. Cf. Felder, *Christ and the Critics,* I, 42.

the Gospels is corroborated by several historical observations
which deal with the condition of the text in the period from
c. 60 A.D. to c. 150 A.D.

The more diffused a writing is the more difficult will it be
for corruptions to creep into the text in the process of tran-
scription. If a text is widely diffused, corruptions will be quickly noticed and localized. Now there are several indications that
the Gospels were wide-spread even during the first half of the
Second Century.

1. There is clear evidence that in the first half of the Second Century, the rank and file of the Christians were acquainted with the Gospels. This is gathered from a statement
which St. Justin M. makes in his First Apology. He says that
it was the practice of the time to read the Gospels to the people every Sunday during services.

For the Apostles in the records which they have made and which
are called the Gospels, have declared that Jesus commanded them
to do as follows. "He took bread and gave thanks and said, Do this
in commemoration of Me."[7]

And on the day which is called Sunday, there is an assembly in the
same place of all who live in cities or in country districts, and the
records of the Apostles . . . are read as long as there is time.[8]

For this practice to take place, it was necessary for the Gospels to have spread in manuscript form among the Christian
communities.

The testimony of Justin the Martyr proves the diffusion of
the Gospels in the Greek language among the Greek speaking
peoples of the eastern part of the Empire. But it can also be
proved that the same Gospels were wide spread in Latin translations among the Latin speaking peoples of the western part
of the Empire as early as the first decades of the Second Century. Some scholars hold that the Latin translations date from

7. I *Apology* 66. 3.
8. *Ibid.,* 67. 3.

the First Century. We read in authentic documents that Proconsul Saturninus of Numidia during the trial of the celebrated twelve martyrs of the tiny town of Scillium ordered that the Scriptures written in Latin be surrendered for burning. This trial was held on July 17, 180 A.D. The order regarding the surrendering of the Scriptures was not peculiar to the trial of the Scillian Martyrs. It was a common order in the trial of Christians and it proves two things. If the Gospels had not been widely diffused and if they did not play an important part in the instruction and formation of Christians—the latter spurs on the former—the pagan authorities would never have demanded their surrender.

We have seen how the existence of Latin translations of the original Greek Gospels doubles the strength of our conclusion that these writings were widely diffused in the Second Century. This conclusion is again emphasized with the evidence of Syriac translations of the same period.[9] Syriac was spoken by a considerable number of Christians of the Levant. Some reputable scholars prefer to think that Tatian's Diatesseron was originally composed in Syriac. Its use in Syriac Christian literature is well known.

2. The group of fourteen writings known as the Apostolic Fathers (composed between c. 70 A.D. and 155 A.D.) gives valuable information concerning the spread of the Gospels. Scholars disagree on the exact place of composition of some of these writings but they are all agreed that they were written in widely separated parts of the ancient world. For example, St. Ignatius (d. 107 A.D.) was from Syrian Antioch; the First Epistle of Clement proceeds from the Christian community of Rome to the Christian community of Corinth (96/98 A.D.); St. Polycarp of Smyrna (d. 155/166 A.D.) in Asia Minor wrote a letter

9. Two famous Syriac MSS of the New Testament are in existence. One is the Curetonian Syriac found by John Cureton in 1858 in a Coptic monastery in the Valley of Nitri which is west of Cairo. The second is the Sinaitic Syriac found by Lewis and Gibson in 1892 on Mt. Sinai. Both date from the Fifth Century. The second is not to be confused with the Greek Sinaiticus found by Tischendorf in the same place.

to the Christian community in Philippi in Macedonia. In spite of the fact that the diffusion of a writing was a slow process in this period, the Apostolic Fathers give unmistakable evidence of being acquainted with all the Gospels.[10] These writings, which, apart from Pastor Hermas, are brief compositions, contain nearly a hundred quotations or echoes from the Gospels. It is believed that the oldest of these writings is the Didache. Several reputable scholars[11] assign this work to a period between 70 A.D. and 100 A.D. There are some thirty direct and indirect quotations or references to the Gospels in this brief composition. The references to the Gospels found in these writings must have been found in a larger writing because it is difficult to see how these references could have penetrated into the different parts of the ancient world if they were not part of a larger writing.

3. One should not overlook the significance of the writings of Papias in a discussion on the integrity of the Gospels. Papias, bishop of Hieropolis in Asia Minor, lived and wrote in the first quarter of the Second Century. This writer not only called two, and probably three, of the Gospels by name in the course of his writings, but also wrote five books of expositions on the Gospels. These expositions were extant in the time of Eusebius of Caesarea (d. 339/340 A.D.). The fact that Papias knew of several of the Gospels at such an early date is some indication of the rapidity of their diffusion.

4. Text scholars have attached a considerable amount of importance to the findings in Egypt of a papyrus fragment of the Fourth Gospel, which has been dated c. 140 A.D.[12] This

10. In his *Institutiones Introductoriae in Libros N.T.* (Rome, 1922), p. 15, Rosadini has a valuable table showing how many times each of the Apostolic Fathers quotes from the Gospels. It proves that all four Gospels were widely diffused from the very beginning.

11. Cayre, *Manual of Patrology,* trans. by Howitt (Tournai, 1936), I, 44.

12. Kenyon, *The John Rylands Library Fragments of the Gospel of St. John* 138–150 A.D., Manchester.

fact has significance regarding the diffusion and consequently the integrity of the Gospels. For even a fragment of the Fourth Gospel to be found in Egypt within a generation after the autograph was written at Ephesus shows that this Gospel was rapidly diffused after it was written.

"The category of Papyri has added a new chapter to textual history and has gone far to bridge the gap between the autographs of the New Testament and the great vellum uncials. There are 53 extant papyri in the official list. Some are small; others considerably large; all of them have the collective value, indicating what types of texts were current in Egypt in the early years of the Christian Church."[13]

5. The oldest extant writing which extensively defends the integrity of the Gospels is Tertullian's *Adversus Marcionem* written about 207/211 A.D. Marcion was a Gnostic who accepted only the Third Gospel, and that only when he had interpolated it to fit his doctrines.[14] Tertullian's refutation pointed out that all the Gospels were integral because at an early date measures were taken to insure the agreement of the transcriptions with the originals.[15]

The observations which are summarized in this chapter warrant the inquirer to conclude that the Gospels have come down to modern times in essentially the same textual condition that they had in the earliest times. The evidence which supports their integrity is great. The number of ancient manuscripts upon which are based the modern critical editions is much greater and much nearer the autographs in point of years than are the manuscripts supporting the integrity of any of the Latin or Greek classics. This is demonstrated by the following diagram:

13. Kenyon, *Our Bible and the Ancient Manuscripts* (New York; Harpers, 1941), p. 98.

14. St. Irenaeus, *Adversus Haereses* Bk. III. 1. 1.

15. Tertullian, *Adversus Marcionem* Bk. IV. 4. 5. Cf. also Eusebius *H.E.* Bk. V. xxviii. 18; and St. Irenaeus, *Adversus Haereses* Bk. IV. 32.

LATIN AUTHORS

Author	Work	Manuscript	Place of MS	Date of MS
Caesar	Gallic Wars	Codex A	Amsterdam	9th–10th C.
		R	Vatican	10th C.
(100–44 BC)		B & M	Paris	9th–11th C.
	Civil Wars	Laurentianus	Florence	10th C.
		Lovaniensis	Louvain	11th C.
Cicero	De Republica	Vaticanus n. 5757	Rome	5th–6th C.
(90–43 BC)	Philippics	7 mss.		11th–13th C.
	Pro Officiis	Ambrosianus	Milan	10th C.
		Harleianus	Harlaam, Holland	9th C.
Horace	Ars Poetica	Parisianus	Paris	10th C.
(65–8 BC)	Satires	Ambrosianus	Milan	10th C.
	Epistles	Bernensis	Bern, Switz.	9th C.
Livy	History of Rome	Veronensis	Verona	4th C.
(57 BC–17 AD)		Parisianus	Paris	10th C.
		All others		10th–15th C.
Ovid	Heroides	Parisianus	Paris	11th C.
(43 BC–17 AD)		Vindobonensis	Vienna	12th C.
Plautus	Comedies	Ambrosianus	Milan	11th C.
(225–184 BC)		Palatinus		10th C.
		Heidelbergensis	Heidelberg	11th C.
Pliny the	Letters	Florentine	Florence	10th C.
Younger		Laurentianus	Florence	10th–11th C.
(62–115 AD)		Dresdensis	Dresden	15th C.
Vergil	Aeneid	Mediceus	Florence	5th C.
(70–19 BC)		Palatinus		10th C.

GREEK AUTHORS

Author	Work	Manuscript	Place of MS	Date of MS
Aeschines	On the Embassy	26 mss.		10th–16th C.
(390–315 BC)	Against Ctesiphon			
Aeschylus	7 Extant Plays	Medicianus	Florence	10th–11th C.
(525–455 BC)				
Aristotle	Parva Naturalia	Parisianus	Paris	10th C.
(384–322 BC)		Vaticanus	Rome	11th C.

GREEK AUTHORS

Herodotus (484–425 BC)	History	Laurentianus Romanus	Florence Rome	10th C. 11th C.
Homer (9th C. BC)	Iliad	Ambrosianus San Marco	Milan Venice	5th–6th C. 10th C.
	Odyssey	Laurentianus Ambrosianus	Florence Milan	10th C. 13th C.
Plato (428–347 BC)	Republic	Parisianus Graecus Venetus Vindobonensis	Paris Venice Vienna	9th C. 12th C. 14th C.
Thucydides (471–396 BC)	History of the Peloponnesian Wars	Italus Vaticanus Laurentianus Palatinus	Paris Rome Florence Heidelberg	11th–12th C. 11th C. 11th C. 11th C.
Xenophon (431–355 BC)	Anabasis	Parisianus N1640 Parisianus N1641	Paris Paris	14th C. 15th C.
	Memorabilia	Parisianus N1302 Parisianus N1642 Laurentianus	Paris Paris Florence	13th C. 15th C. 13th C.
Gospels in Greek (written c. 60-100 AD)		**Chester Beatty Pap. Cod.**	**London**	**3rd C.**
		Vaticanus	**Rome**	**4th C.**
		Sinaiticus	**London**	**4th-5th C.**
		Alexandrinus	**London**	**5th C.**
		Ephraemi (palimpsest)	**Paris**	**5th C.**
		Bezae Cantabrigiensis	**Cambridge**	**5th C.**
		Rossanenis	**Calabria, Italy**	**6th C.**
		Beratinus	**Berat, Albania**	**6th C.**

"The authenticity of the Four Gospels has enormously more testimony than can be collected for any of the Greek and Latin classics."[16] And we might add that if the New Testament text scholar has any difficulty in his work it is not because he has too little material to work with but because he has too much. The situation is exactly reversed in the case of scholars collecting ancient documents of classical works. That difficulty verges

16. Dom John Chapman, *The Four Gospels* (New York; Sheed & Ward, 1944), p. 5.

on despair in the case of Lucretius' *De Rerum Natura* for which there are only three Ninth Century manuscripts or Sallust's *Bellum Catilinae* which is supported by only four Tenth and Eleventh Century manuscripts and Longinus's *On the Sublime* for which there is only one manuscript of the Fifteenth Century. We are conscious of the part that the papyrus fragments found in recent years, especially at Oxyrhynchus and Tebtunis in Egypt, can play in the text of the pagan classics.

VI

The Authorship of the Gospels

External Evidence

AN INQUIRY into the authorship of a writing is an important
one because many times it permits the inquirer to determine
in what position the author was to know the truth of the events
which he recorded. But one is cautioned against thinking that
the author of a work can be definitely known only when his
name appears in the writing. This is certainly not the case.
Scholars can prove the authorship of many writings in which
the author's name does not appear. They can also prove that
many a writing was not written by the person whose name is
appended to it.

It was shown in the last chapter that the Gospels have been
integral from the earliest times. They were extensively used
by Christians as early as the Second Century. But even while
the Gospels were being used, there began to appear certain
false gospels known as the apocryphal gospels. Some of these
false gospels are extant today. The names of about twenty of
them are still known[1] and it is certain that a great many more
have been lost. The very existence and nature of these apocryphal gospels shed some light on the authentic Gospels.

The apocryphal gospels presuppose the existence of the authentic Gospels for they are based on them and claim to sup-

1. Cayre, *Manual of Patrology* (Tournai, 1936), I, 159ff.

plement the information contained in them. The imitation is completed when Apostles or persons close to Christ are claimed as the authors of these works. Since the apocryphal gospels of the Second Century were based on the authentic Gospels, it follows that the authentic Gospels go back to an earlier period and were actually written by persons close to Christ. The composers of the apocryphal gospels, realizing that the authentic Gospels were well entrenched in Christian practices, probably knew that their own narratives would never be accepted if they were not closely patterned after the authentic Gospels in content and authorship.

It would be wrong to think that all the apocryphal gospels were composed to sow error. Some merely contained a series of pious stories intended to edify the faithful. They are, however, truly apocryphal writings because they were ascribed to persons close to Christ. Some of the stories which were doctrinally harmless had considerable influence in early Christian art and found their way into a writing no less famous than Dante's *Divine Comedy*.[2]

The presence of apocryphal gospels among the Christians in the Second Century made it imperative to find a basis on which to distinguish the true Gospels from the false gospels. In 1740, L. A. Muratori found in the Ambrosian Library in Milan an ancient document which proves that in the Second Century definite means were taken to insure that the apocryphal gospels were not confounded with the authentic ones. This literary fragment contained a list of the writings which the Christians of about 165 A.D. were to regard as genuine. Its beginning and end are missing but it does say that Luke wrote the third authentic Gospel and John the fourth. If it had not been mutilated it would no doubt tell us that the other two were written by Matthew and Mark. It is important to notice that the time of the appearance of this canon fits in perfectly with what we

2. It is in an early apocryphal *Acts of the Apostles* that we find the story of *Quo Vadis*.

know of the state of affairs during this period. It was in the Second Century when apocryphal writings began to appear in considerable numbers, and with their appearance there increased the danger that they might be confused with the genuine Gospels. To prevent this state of affairs from developing, this list or canon of the authentic Gospels was drawn up.

The Ante-Nicene writers leave no doubt that the authentic Gospels were distinguished from the apocryphal gospels by the names of the Evangelists who were associated with the Gospels. In this way, as more copies of the originals were made and diffused, the names of the Evangelists became better known. Since the Gospels were widely spread in the Second Century, so were the names of the Evangelists widely known. We shall cite the testimony of three writers of the first three centuries who were well acquainted with the tradition concerning the names of the Evangelists.

Tertullian of Carthage (c. 150–220) knew the tradition of his time, appealing to it repeatedly in his controversies with the Gnostics. He states that an authentic tradition must go back to the beginnings of Christianity and tells his opponents where they can find such a tradition. The tradition which Tertullian knew concerning the authorship of the Gospels is set down in his work entitled *Adversus Marcionem*. This work is extant today and the passage pertinent to the authorship of the Gospels reads as follows:

We affirm, first of all, that the source of proof which the Gospels furnish indicates the Apostles to be their own authors. . . . I maintain that this Gospel of Luke existed from the very beginning of its publication in the Apostolic churches and in all those which were united to them through a common bond of faith, while that of Marcion was unknown to most of the congregations and if known to any was bitterly condemned. The same authority of the Apostolic churches also supports the other Gospels which we possess through them and after them . . . namely the Gospels of John

and Matthew as well as the Gospel of Mark which is designated as
that of Peter whose interpreter Mark was.[3]

St. Irenaeus of Lyons (c. 140–202/203) in Gaul was in a
peculiarly favorable position to know the truth of the tradition regarding the authorship of the Gospels. He was acquainted with the traditions of the East and the West. He was
born in Asia Minor and spent some time in study there. He
also knew the tradition of the West for he succeeded Pothinus
(d. 177/178) as the bishop of Lyons. Besides this, he explicitly
states that he set out to discover personally the tradition of
Rome. While St. Irenaeus was in Asia Minor, he was the disciple of St. Polycarp of Smyrna (155/156) who in turn was a
disciple of St. John the Apostle.[4] In Lyons he learned the
ancient tradition of this region from Pothinus who was about
ninety years old when he was martyred. The fruit of Irenaeus'
travel and study regarding the authorship of the Gospels is
summed up in a passage of his work against the Gnostics. In
that passage he states:

Matthew published his Gospel among the Hebrews and in their
own language at the time when Peter and Paul were preaching the
glad tidings in Rome and founding the church there. After departure Mark also, the pupil and interpreter of Peter, has given
us what has been preached. Luke, however, a companion of Paul,
has chronicled in his work the Gospel as it was preached by that
Apostle. After that John, the disciple of the Lord, who was reclin-
ing on his breast, published his Gospel while he was residing at
Ephesus in Asia.[5]

Irenaeus then adds that this knowledge was the universal
tradition of the Church.[6]

3. *Adversus Marcionem* Bk. IV. 5. MPG Vol. II, Col. 365. *De Praescriptione Haereticorum* 32.
4. *Adversus Haereses* III. 3. 6.
5. *Adversus Haereses* III. 1. 1. MPG Vol. VII, Col. 844.
6. *Adversus Haereses* III. 11. 8.

The student does well to consider the testimony of Origen (c. 185–254/255 A.D.) of Alexandria in Egypt regarding the authorship of the Gospels. Origen was undoubtedly one of the most erudite men of the Ante-Nicene Period. His interest and contributions to Scripture studies are well-known. Furthermore, he was also in a favorable position to learn personally the ancient tradition concerning the authorship of the Gospels. He succeeded Clement as head of the Catechetical School of Alexandria. Clement, in turn, was taught by men of olden times who came from many parts of the Greek-speaking world. Origen's testimony regarding the authorship of the Gospels is summarized in his first commentary on Matthew. In it he states that he,

learned from tradition concerning the four Gospels which alone are unquestionable in the Church of God under heaven, that first was written that according to Matthew, who was once a tax collector, but afterwards an Apostle of Jesus Christ, who published it for those who from Judaism came to believe, composed as it was in the Hebrew language. Secondly, that according to Mark, who wrote according to Peter's instructions. . . . Thirdly, that according to Luke, who wrote for those who from the Gentiles came to believe, the Gospel that was preached by Paul. After them all, that according to John.[7]

The conclusion must be drawn from these three important Ante-Nicene writers that the authors of the four accepted Gospels were Matthew, Mark, Luke and John. The firmness of this conclusion is thrown into greater relief when one notices that these references were taken from writers who together reflect the tradition of the principal geographical sections of the ancient world. But it must not be thought that this conclusion rests only on these three passages. Scores of similar passages

7. Quoted by Eusebius in H. E. (Bk. VI. xxv. 4–6), trans. by Lake & Oulton in Loeb Classical Library (London; Heinemann, 1926). Used with permission of Harvard University Press.

from these and other writers could be produced to support the same conclusion.

These quotations were selected because the names of all four Evangelists are included in a single passage and because their authors were in a favorable position to know the truth of the tradition which they have recorded.

Internal Evidence

It is extremely difficult if not impossible to determine who the Evangelists were by the reading of their writings alone. In the first place, none of the four authentic Gospels contains the name of its author. Then, too, biographical details which might refer to the author are not definite enough to point to any particular person. It is true that the Gospels clearly show that their authors were well acquainted with the political and religious conditions of their time. They knew the legal procedures, the customs and prejudices of the Jews. They had first hand knowledge of the geography of the Holy Land. But the most that this proves is that the Evangelists were observant contemporaries of Christ and residents of Palestine. The information that we have just listed was not the exclusive property of these four men. It was knowledge common to many people. Internal evidence alone, then, does not produce conclusive proof concerning the authorship of the Gospels.

It would be a serious mistake, however, to think that an internal investigation of the Gospels would be fruitless in producing information to corroborate evidence derived from external sources. Although we can prove conclusively who the Evangelists were from the works of early writers, we can show from the Gospels themselves that these ancient authors were correct in their testimony. In conjunction with the statements of the ancients, the force of the internal arguments is considerable and certainly not to be disregarded.

Matthew—Early Christian tradition (St. Irenaeus, Clement

of Alexandria, Origen, Eusebius and others) is agreed that not only did St. Matthew write the First Gospel, but also that he directed it to the Jews. They state that it was originally written in the Aramaic language and was intended either to strengthen converts from Judaism or to influence prospective ones.

An examination of St. Matthew's Gospel shows that the tradition concerning its purpose is correct. Its theme is one which only the Jews of that day could fully understand. It is that Jesus is the Messias promised to the Chosen People in the writings of the prophets. To prove his point, Matthew makes abundant use of Old Testament material. He shows how Christ came to found a Messianic kingdom in which all the nations of the earth would have a place. He shows how Christ by his teachings and miracles did all in His power to induce the Jews to accept membership in this kingdom and how they did all they could to nullify His efforts and to erase His memory from history.

Mark—Ancient writers have recorded that the Christians of Rome, seeing that Mark had long been associated with Peter, asked him to write an account of the Apostle's preaching since he was in a favorable position to do so. They say that when Mark completed his work, he presented it to Peter for approval before giving it to the people.

There are several indications in the Second Gospel which justify our acceptance of the tradition that Mark was closely associated with Peter in Rome. (A) Peter is mentioned twenty-four times in St. Mark's Gospel, but unlike in the other Gospels, he is never pictured in a favorable light, thus showing that Mark instead of interjecting his own admiration for his master, wrote as Peter in his humility preached. (B) Mark refers to Rufus and Alexander, the sons of Simon of Cyrene, in a way which seems to indicate that they were well known to his readers. It is indeed striking that in the Epistle to the Romans, St. Paul speaks of a Rufus and an Alexander as being residents of Rome. (C) It is clear that this Gospel was not directed toward the Jews because it is singularly free from references to Jewish customs and Old Testament prophecies. On the other hand, the casualness with which he uses such latinisms as "pretorian," "census," "denarius" and "tribute to Caesar" shows that the author felt no need to explain these terms to his readers.

Luke—The explicit testimony of antiquity (Muratorian Canon, Clement of Alexandria, St. Justin the Martyr, Origen and others) informs us that the Third Gospel was written by St. Luke, a Gentile, a physician and a close associate of St. Paul. It was directed to the non-Jewish converts to Christianity.

An examination of the Third Gospel produces this information: (A) The grammar of this Gospel proves that its author was a Gentile. That the other three Evangelists were Jews is indicated by their use of grammatical constructions that are peculiar to their Aramaic language. The same cannot be said of Luke. He is familiar with a syntactic language, whereas, the others are most familiar with the paratactic language of the Jews. (B) Three times does St. Paul refer to his association with "Luke, the beloved physician." Luke refers to his association with St. Paul in the "we" passages in his Acts of the Apostles. (C) In his writings, Luke shows an unusual interest in the diseases cured by Christ. The terms he uses to describe them are not those of a layman, but they are technical terms used by men of the medical profession. (D) We see that Luke was writing for the benefit of Gentiles from the fact that he stresses those episodes in Christ's life which give hope to the Gentiles. He repeatedly states that Christ is the Savior of all and not only of the Jews. His kingdom is open to all.

The tradition that St. Luke was an artist is not very reliable. It first appeared in the Sixth Century in the writings of Theodore of Constantinople.

John—Of the four Evangelists, the author of the last Gospel most clearly reveals his identity in his writing. On several occasions, he calls himself "the disciple whom Jesus loved." The

Gospels tells us that the three disciples especially favored by Christ were Peter, James and John. Of these three, the "beloved disciple" could not have been James for he had been dead many years when this work was written. It was not Peter for, on two occasions, the Evangelist makes a clear distinction[8] between himself and Peter. The process of elimination leaves John to be the author of the Fourth Gospel.

St. Irenaeus[9] who was taught by St. Polycarp who, in turn, was a disciple of St. John the Evangelist says that the last Gospel was written at Ephesus in Asia. He goes on to say that in this city toward the year 100 A.D. there appeared a group of heretics known as Cerinthians who denied the divinity of Christ; they held that Christ was but the first creature of God. St. Irenaeus tells us that John wrote his Gospel to crush this error.

Although the divinity of Christ can be proved from any of the Gospels, the last one especially stresses it. It opens with the words: "The Word was God" and closes with the summary verse reading, "These were written that you may believe that Jesus is the Christ, the Son of God."[10] John's readers were not Jews—Ephesus was a Greek city—for he is constrained to explain Jewish customs and to translate Aramaic words. They seem to have been people who had been evangelized some time ago, but whose faith had to be bolstered in the face of the Cerinthian threat.

The external evidence which points to Matthew, Mark, Luke and John as the authors of the Gospels is abundant and conclusive. The internal evidence although insufficient in itself is a strong confirmation of the correctness of the ancient tradition regarding the identity of the Evangelists.

8. Jn. 20:2; 21:7, 20.
9. *Adv. Haer.* I. 26. 1.
10. Jn. 20:31.

VII

The Historicity of the Gospels

WHEN THE INTEGRITY and authorship of the Gospels has been established, the student is warranted to take the next step in the inquiry into the value of the Gospels: an investigation of their historicity. The aim of this search is to discover whether or not the events which are recorded in these writings actually took place. The same criteria will be applied to the Gospels to test their historicity as are applied to any profane historical document.

Perhaps this question comes most spontaneously to the mind of one investigating the historical value of the Gospels: "Were Matthew, Mark, Luke and John in a position to know the truth of the events which they recorded in the Gospels?" For an answer to this pointed question, the inquirer is referred to the Ante-Nicene writers who were qualified to give it. Their answer is valid because they were personally familiar with ancient and controlled tradition concerning the Evangelists. Many quotations from these writers could be produced which are pertinent to the question under consideration, but limitations of space permit only two quotations for each Evangelist:

Matthew

... of the Twelve Apostles and Seventy Disciples. . . . Yet nevertheless of all those who had been with the Lord only Matthew and

John have left their recollections and tradition says that they took
to writing perforce. . . .[1]

. . . The First (Gospel) that was written was according to Matthew who was once a tax collector but afterwards an Apostle of
Jesus Christ.[2]

Mark

But the hearers of Peter . . . with every kind of exhortation besought Mark . . . whose Gospel is extant, seeing that he was Peter's
follower . . . to leave them a written statement of the teaching
given them verbally . . . and they say that the Apostle . . . was
pleased with their zeal and ratified the Scripture for study in the
churches. Clement quotes this story in the 6th book of Hypotyposes
and Papias confirms him.[3]

Mark became Peter's interpreter and wrote accurately all that
he remembered. . . . He had not seen the Lord . . . but later on
followed Peter. Mark did nothing wrong in writing down single
points as he remembered them, for to one thing he gave attention,
to leave nothing out of what he had heard and to make no false
statements in them. This is related by Papias about Mark.[4]

Luke

Luke himself . . . felt obliged to release us from the doubtful
propositions of others and related in his own Gospel the accurate
account of the things of which he had himself firmly learned the
truth from his profitable association with Paul and his conversation with the other Apostles.[5]

For even Luke's form of the Gospel men usually ascribe to Paul.[6]

1. *H.E.* III. xxiv. 5.
2. Origen, *Comm. in Matt. H.E.* VI. xxv. 3.
3. *H.E.* II. xv. 2.
4. *H.E.* III. xxxix. 15.
5. *H.E.* III. xxiv. 15.
6. *Adv. Marc.* Bk. IV. 5.

John

Then John the disciple of the Lord who had even rested upon His breast, himself also gave forth the Gospel.[7]

Why need I speak of him who leaned back on Jesus' breast, John who has left behind him one Gospel?[8]

It is quite evident that the Evangelists were in ideal circumstances to know the truth of the events which they recorded in the Gospels. Matthew and John, being Apostles of Christ, were eye-witnesses of these events. Since Mark was a disciple of Peter the Apostle, his Gospel also has eye-witness value. And there is evidence that Luke, though not an Apostle, received his information from several sources close to Christ. One source was Paul who was intimately associated with the Apostles; other sources were certain eye-witnesses whose veracity he checked.[9]

Pascal once said that he would only believe the person who was willing to die for what he said. The inference is that no sane person suffers for what he knows to be a falsehood when he can live in peace by telling the truth. It is true that one might suffer for certain social or political principles which he thinks are correct, but no one willingly suffers to propagate as historical, events which never took place. Now both Peter and Paul, whose preaching is recorded in the Gospels of Mark and Luke, suffered and died[10] to propagate doctrines which are essentially bound up with historical occurrences. John the Evangelist was exiled to the island of Patmos[11] in the Aegean Sea "for the word of God and the testimony of Jesus."[12] But persecution could not force the Evangelists to deviate from

7. St. Irenaeus, *Adv. Her.* III. i. 1.
8. Origen, *Comm. in Ioa.* H.E. VI. xxv. 9–10.
9. Luke 1:2.
10. Tertullian, *Adv. Marc.* Bk. IV. 5; also *H.E.* II. xxv. 5–8.
11. *H.E.* III. xviii. 1.
12. Apoc. 1:2.

their historical theme, for this theme is the same in the first three Gospels, which were written about 65 A.D., as it is in St. John's Gospel, which was written toward the year 100 A.D. The theme of all the Gospels was to project the historical personality of Christ into the future. It can be concluded, then, that not only did the Evangelists know the truth about Christ, but they also wished to tell it.

Some critics have commented that, since the Evangelists were uneducated men, they could not be depended upon to report faithfully the events of the Gospels. Analysis shows that this objection is more apparent than real. Education and even specialized training are required to be able to glean historical truth from complex or fragmentary sources or from archeological discoveries. Much reading and experience is needed to be able to evaluate or trace accurately the ramifications of events. But this was certainly not required of the Evangelists for them to know the truth of the events which they recorded in the Gospels. All they had to do to know the truth was to keep their eyes on one Person, namely, Christ, and then to re-tell some of the occurrences in which He was the central figure. This is an easy task for even an uneducated person. In fact, it was easier for the Evangelists to know the truth of the events of the Gospels than it is for a war correspondent to know and report precisely the progress of a military campaign because the latter is much more complex than the former.

The observations of the several preceding paragraphs, which show that not only were the Evangelists well able to know the truth concerning the events of the Gospels but also wished to record them as they knew them, constitute the essence of the discussion on the historicity of the Gospels. But there are several points which are well worth examining in this connection.

Christianity, or the religion of the Gospels, is very different from any ancient or modern non-Christian religion. One of the points of dissimilarity lies in the fact that Christianity is essentially bound up with the Person of its Founder, while it is conceivable for a non-Christian religion to be propagated without anything being said of its originator. In a non-Christian religion, the emphasis could be placed on the sayings of the founder and not on the events of his life. This is not the case with the religion of the Gospels. That religion is so bound up with an historical Person that a student would miss the essence of Christianity if he neglected to study its Founder. From this it can be seen that the nature of Christianity in reality compels a convert to learn the truth about Christ. In the first decades of the Christian Era, this entailed an investigation into the truth of the Gospels, which were purposely written to project the personality of Christ into the future.

The task of investigating the truth of the events of the Gospels was not a difficult one. The existence and the activities of Christ were widely known. The details of Christ's life were public for the most part and were of such a nature as to attract the attention of the highest officials of Judaism, of several petty kings, of a Roman procurator, of the best known contemporary Jewish writer, Josephus, and of one of the best known Latin pagan historians of ancient times, Tacitus. Furthermore, these events were recorded in the Gospels when a great many persons who actually witnessed them were still alive. Persons who were already adults when Christ died, were but from fifty to sixty-five years old when the first three Gospels were written; and some ancient writers cite instances of certain exceptional eye-witnesses who lived until after the writing of the Gospel of St. John.

The Gospels themselves suggest that their contents were well-known by the people. This can be gathered from the fact that the tone of the Gospels is one of a summary of things already known and not that of a writing which is telling of things for the first time. Even though Christ died during the procuratorship of Pontius Pilate (25–35 A.D.), it must not be thought that the details of His life were permitted to drop out of the consciousness of men until the time when the Gospels were written. A spoken Gospel preceded the written Gospels by as much as twenty-five years. It is this spoken or preached Gospel which is summarized in the Gospels written by the four Evangelists.

The events of the Gospels were a stumbling block to belief for the Jews. The Jews were unwilling to accept such a Messias as the Gospels pictured. They wanted a Messias who would liberate them from the Roman yoke and make Jerusalem the political and cultural center of the world. But the Gospels portrayed the Messias as one who did not care for earthly kingdoms and who even predicted the destruction of Jerusalem. Naturally, then, the decisive means at the disposal of the Jews by which they could replace their deeply embedded, popular notion of the Messias with the notion of the spiritual Messias of the Gospels was to investigate thoroughly the truth of the spoken and written Gospels. Yet it can be proved that many Jews[13] became Christians.

The pagans considered it foolishness to pay homage and allegiance to a Person who seemed too helpless to prevent men from putting Him to death in such a disgraceful way as crucifixion. To become a member of the religion founded by Christ meant that one would have to live with the possibility either of losing his property by confiscation, or of martyrdom continually imminent. Naturally speaking, how could these pagans bring themselves to accept Christ and the consequences of being His followers? The principal means by which this could be accomplished was by an investigation into the truth and claims of Christ as they were outlined in the Gospels. Even pagan sources show that many were converted to Christianity.[14]

There is conclusive evidence that the early Christians did

13. *H.E.* VI. xxv. 4.

14. Tacitus, *Annales* Bk. XV. 44; Pliny, *Ep. 96 ad Trajani*, Letters Bk. 10.

investigate the truth of the written Gospels. This can be gathered from their attitude toward the apocryphal gospels. The authors of the apocrypha, seeing the influence which the authentic Gospels already had upon the people, composed these forged gospels hoping that they would have a similar influence. This explains why the apocryphal gospels were patterned after the authentic Gospels in contents and authorship. Now since these two types of gospels were similar, one would expect to find them both accepted by the early Christians. However, the apocrypha were generally rejected, while the Gospels of Matthew, Mark, Luke, and John were accepted. The ultimate reason for this decisive action must have been that the contents and authorship of both groups were investigated but one was found to be false and was rejected while the other was accepted as trustworthy.

The arguments sketched herein are premises which fully justify the conclusion that the Gospels are historical documents. Each of these particular arguments was chosen because it is applicable to the Gospels as a whole. It is impossible in the space available to list and discuss the parallels of Gospel events as they are found in ancient literature, nor is it possible here to show how many Gospel details are corroborated by archeological discoveries. Suffice it to say that whenever historical sciences have made discoveries which touched upon the Gospels, the Gospels have been proved to be trustworthy.

Theories of Critics

The student may be led to appreciate better the effectiveness of the positive arguments for the historicity of the Gospels by examining the negative arguments for it. By "negative arguments" is meant the fruitlessness of the labors of critics who for various reasons have attempted to discredit the Gospels as historical documents. An implicit and explicit conclusion will become apparent as the negative arguments are unfolded. The implicit conclusion will be the great importance which investigators place on the Gospels in the study of Apologetics. These critics regarded the position of the Gospels as fundamental and so have expended an astonishing amount of effort in attempting to disprove them. The explicit conclusion is that despite this great amount of intellectual labor on the part of critics, they have not been able to discover a single valid argument which would weaken the reliability of the Gospels. This failure throws into bolder relief the force of the positive arguments which have just been concluded.

Documents which claim to be historical should be tested according to the rules of historical method. Since the Gospels clearly claim to be accounts of events which have taken place, it follows that they should be examined according to these rules. Rationalist critics reject the trustworthiness of the Gospels even before they begin to test it. But they do not arrive at this rejection by a conscientious application of the rules of historical method. They reject the Gospels because the Gospels contain accounts of miracles and of the supernatural. These phenomena are impossible according to the philosophical—not historical—principles of rationalists. Says Renan:

That the Gospels are partly legend is evident, since they are full of miracles and the supernatural. Not because it has been proven to me that the Gospels are undeserving of an absolute faith in them but because they relate miracles do I say, "The Gospels are legends."[15]

Says Boussett:

Every absolutely marvelous, wholly incomprehensible event . . . and everything inscrutable shows itself in advance according to its subject matter to be dogmatic legend.[16]

15. Quoted by Felder in *Christ and the Critics,* trans. by J. L. Stoddard (London; Burns, Oates and Washbourne Ltd., 1924) I, 112.
16. *Ibid.*

The illogical procedure of the critics is apparent at once. Instead of applying the rules of historical method to the Gospels, the critics apply false philosophical principles to them.[17] Their conclusion is drawn before the investigation begins. With the major premise that miracles are impossible, the conclusion must be that the Gospels are not historical. These critics show themselves ready to modify the facts with their theory, whereas a theory should be modified by the facts.

This brief explanation permits one to interpret better the points of view and the underlying themes of the theories about to be discussed.

1. *Deception Theory* (Reimarus, 1694–1768)

The deception theory holds that the Gospels were composed to bolster a fraud started by the Apostles. It depicts Christ as a Jew who wished to free the Jewish people from the Roman yoke. He is assumed to have chosen the Apostles as His co-plotters. This scheme won the sympathy of some people who saw to it that Christ and His accomplices wanted for nothing. Then, according to this theory, the plot was discovered, Christ was put to death and His associates dispersed. But after Christ's death, the Apostles, who had become used to easy living, were reluctant to return to their former occupations of manual labor. How could they continue to live in this luxury? According to this theory, the Apostles set out on a campaign of mass deception to achieve their ends. They sublimated Christ by transforming Him from a person ambitious for earthly power to a heavenly redeemer who offered hope to men. The Apostles knew that they could find enough simpletons who would believe it and, incidentally, continue to support them. The Gospels are supposed to have been written to bolster this huge

17. The false philosophical principles are that miracles and supernatural occurrences are impossible on earth. They are not impossible for there is nothing contradictory about them from the standpoint of God, or man, or the things themselves.

fraud and so must themselves be frauds. So wrote Reimarus.
Several comments should be made on the deception theory
of Reimarus. It must be remarked that there is nothing in the
Gospels or in the rest of the New Testament or in any un-
prejudiced ancient writer which supports it. In fact, the Gospels show that Christ never cared for earthly kingdoms, that
it was not the Apostles but Christ who proclaimed Himself to
be a Redeemer; that the Apostles did return to their former
occupations, and that the learned, as well as the unlearned,
were attracted by the preaching of Christ.

Reimarus's deception theory was destroyed by his own fellow critics such as Strauss and Schweitzer, and today it is only
of historical interest for it has been defunct for years.

2. *Natural Explanation Theory* (Paulus, d. 1851)

The natural explanation theory accepts the Gospels as historical but it holds that men misinterpret them when they say
that they contain accounts of miracles and of the supernatural.
This theory would interpret the Gospels thus so that their miraculous and supernatural elements could not be distinguished
from their natural elements. It claims that if all the information about a given Gospel miracle were known, that event
would not appear to be miraculous. The proponents of this
theory then proceed to supply the supposedly missing information. When they have eliminated every vestige of the supernatural from the Gospels, they then accept them as historical.

The natural explanation theory is a good illustration of the
unwillingness of critics to accept the miraculous and the supernatural and of the lengths to which they will go to eliminate it. The critics should have listed the sources from which
they derived the "information" which they use to make the
supernatural elements of the Gospels fade into the natural.
They are not able to explain satisfactorily why the Evangelists
who were close to the events of the Gospels did not record
them as natural if they really were natural occurrences.

3. *The Myth Theory* (Strauss 1808–1874)

Strauss put the Gospels on a par with pagan mythologies, stating that they had their origin in the same manner, that is to say, in the imagination of the people, and as such could command no degree of credibility. Strauss knew well that it takes time for facts to assume the trappings of myths and so was forced by his own theory to assign the composition of the Gospels to the Second Century. And this assigning of the composition of the Gospels to the Second Century proved to be the weak link in the whole theory, for the evidence of the ante-Nicene literature is overwhelmingly opposed to setting it at such a late date. Every argument in favor of the integrity and authorship of the Gospels is conclusive and is implicitly an argument against this theory.

4. *Evolutionary Theory* (Ritschl, d. 1889)

The evolutionary theory is the most popular one today among rationalistic critics. It was worked out by the Liberal School whose chief exponent was Adolf von Harnack. This is the theory in brief: Christ was a mere man who possessed a powerful personality by which He was able to impress deeply all who came in contact with Him. After His death, His followers were still amazed by the effect He had made upon them and so began to idealize Him. Among the great things which they began to attribute to Him were miracles and, from miracles, it was a short step to making Him divine. According to this theory, Christ's followers were interested in making converts and so they molded their sublimations into didactic writings designed to influence prospective converts. These writings were the Gospels. Those who were responsible for the Gospels cannot be accused of conscious intention to deceive, but they were the innocent victims of an excessive zeal for Christ. In either case the Gospels do not represent objective reality.

The members of this school knew that it takes time to build a myth or a legend and, because Strauss's theory required one hundred and twenty-five years, they rejected it. Yet they them-

HISTORICITY OF GOSPELS

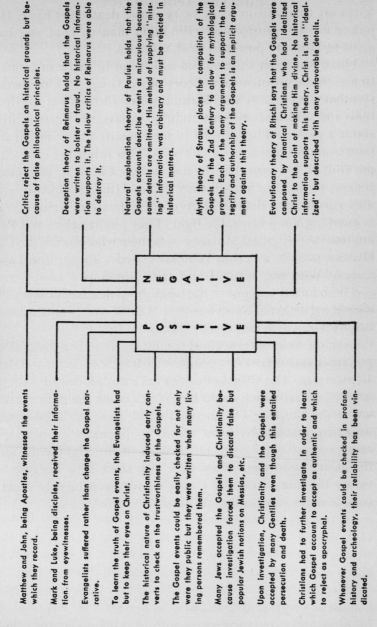

POSITIVE / NEGATIVE

POSITIVE

Matthew and John, being Apostles, witnessed the events which they record.

Mark and Luke, being disciples, received their information from eyewitnesses.

Evangelists suffered rather than change the Gospel narrative.

To learn the truth of Gospel events, the Evangelists had but to keep their eyes on Christ.

The historical nature of Christianity induced early converts to check on the trustworthiness of the Gospels.

The Gospel events could be easily checked for not only were they public but they were written when many living persons remembered them.

Many Jews accepted the Gospels and Christianity because investigation forced them to discard false but popular Jewish notions on Messias, etc.

Upon investigation, Christianity and the Gospels were accepted by many Gentiles even though this entailed persecution and death.

Christians had to further investigate in order to learn which Gospel account to accept as authentic and which to reject as apocryphal.

Whenever Gospel events could be checked in profane history and archeology, their reliability has been vindicated.

NEGATIVE

Critics reject the Gospels on historical grounds but because of false philosophical principles.

Deception theory of Reimarus holds that the Gospels were written to bolster a fraud. No historical information supports it. The fellow critics of Reimarus were able to destroy it.

Natural explanation theory of Paulus holds that the Gospels accounts describe events as miraculous because some details are omitted. His method of supplying "missing" information was arbitrary and must be rejected in historical matters.

Myth theory of Strauss places the composition of the Gospels in the 2nd Century to allow for mythological growth. Each of the many arguments to support the integrity and authorship of the Gospels is an implicit argument against this theory.

Evolutionary theory of Ritschl says that the Gospels were composed by fanatical Christians who had idealized Christ to the point of making Him divine. No historical information supports this theory. Christ is not "idealized" but described with many unfavorable details.

selves say that within forty years of the death of Christ, His followers had transformed Him from man to God and had given to Him the power to work miracles.

There is another observation which can be made in connection with the evolutionary theory of the Gospels. This theory says that the Gospels are idealizations of Christ. But idealizations and sublimations only indulge in favorable generalities about a person. They rarely go into details which might detract from the character of the hero. This is not the case with the Gospels because they do not portray Christ in sweeping, general terms, but rather they depict Him graphically and with a great many details. Many of these details describe Christ in anything but a favorable light. They picture Him as a Person from the despised province of Galilee who was rejected by His own people; a Person Who associated with publicans and sinners; Who was accused and condemned as a blasphemer and Who finally was put to the disgraceful death of crucifixion after being deserted by all but four of those overly enthusiastic followers of which this theory speaks.

From the brief sketches and comments upon the theories of the critics, one is now in a position to draw the conclusion that they warrant. The efforts of critics have not produced a single valid argument which could be urged against the trustworthiness of the Gospels. The theories which were outlined in the preceding paragraphs have waned in popularity since they were propounded by the rationalists of the eighteenth and nineteenth centuries. They were discussed here because in history the attacks on the Gospels have been merely repetitions of these and similar theories with refinements.

VIII

Christ Claimed to be Divine

ONCE THE SOUNDNESS of the Gospels as historical documents has been established, one is justified in searching them for evidence of divine revelation.

The main character of the Gospels is Jesus Christ. He overshadows everything else which these writings contain, because His chief claim was that He was God. He declared His divinity not in the loose, figurative sense of the term, but in its strictly literal sense. He said that He was an Infinite Being having the attributes of power and knowledge in an unlimited degree.

Noticing the arrangement of the material of the Gospels, it is evident that the Evangelists did not intend their writings to be looked upon as logically divided treatises on doctrinal subjects, nor was it their intention to write a life of Christ either in an exhaustive fashion or in strict chronological sequence. All four Evangelists treat but one subject. It is Jesus Christ. He is the only theme of the Gospels. Christ plays the only role. Details which do not refer to Him directly are woven into the text to help the reader to understand Christ better. In short, it must be said that without Christ there would be no Gospels as we know them. The question is, then, "Why do the Evangelists place such great emphasis on Christ? Why is so much attention paid to Him in the Gospels?"

The reason for the overshadowing position of Christ in the Gospels is the fact that He made several claims which astonished and aroused the wonderment of His listeners. These claims are unique in history and, although they were made in various circumstances, they all revolve about the same subject, namely, Christ as He claims to be God.

Christ's "unveiling" of Himself was not an abrupt affair, accomplished all at once. It was rather a gradual unfolding which depended not on Christ's ability to reveal Himself, but on the ability and capacity of His listeners to receive the concepts which He was to impart. It is the purpose of this chapter to consider the principal claim of Christ, and the one which gives meaning to His other claims. In the paragraphs which follow are discussed five instances of Christ's making this claim.

1. In the fifth chapter[1] of St. John's Gospel is recorded an incident which occurred during a visit of Christ to Jerusalem on the occasion of a certain Jewish feast. While in Jerusalem, He happened to pass by a pool near the Sheep Gate. There He noticed a man who had been crippled for thirty-eight years, and, having compassion on him, restored him to health. The Jews, who were watching Jesus, observed this deed and were angered by the fact that it violated the Sabbath rest. Christ sought to explain His action by the statement,

"My Father works even until now, and I work." (John 5:17) The verse which immediately follows this statement records the reaction of the people to these words of Christ. It reads,

This, then, is why the Jews were seeking the more to put him to death; because he was not only breaking the Sabbath, but also calling God His own Father, making Himself equal to God. [John 5:18]

In the narrative which follows this passage, Christ showed that the Jews did not misunderstand Him when they accused Him of claiming to be God; for whenever the Jews misunderstood Him, Christ would correct their mistaken notions. On

1. John 5:1–23.

this occasion, He not only let His statement stand, but added several other statements to re-emphasize His original claim to divinity.

2. The incident involving Christ which St. John relates in the tenth chapter[2] of his Gospel is pertinent to the inquiry now being made. It took place in the Temple at Jerusalem in Solomon's Porch which the doctors of the law used as a place of instruction. One day, while Jesus was there, the Jews put to Him the demand, "If thou art the Christ, tell us openly." Jesus answered them in these words: "I have told you, but you will not believe me." And He concluded His answer with the statement, "My Father and I are one."

When the Jews heard these unmistakable words, they took up stones with which to stone Him to death, giving as their reason,

Not for a good work do we stone Thee, but for blasphemy, and because thou, being a man, makest thyself God. [John 10:33]

If the Jews had mistaken Christ's words as a claim to divinity, Christ certainly had the opportunity to correct their erroneous notions. He did nothing of the sort. Rather He underscored His original claim by appealing to the works which He had performed saying,

If you are not willing to believe me, believe the works, that you may know and believe that the Father is in me and I in the Father. [John 10:38]

When He said this, once again they had a mind to seize Him.

3. The occasion of an incident recorded in the fifth chapter[3] of St. Luke's Gospel was slightly different from the two already considered, but it deals with precisely the same question.

2. John 10:22–40.
3. Luke 5:17–26.

After Christ had acquired a reputation as a teacher, many Pharisees and doctors of the law came from Galilee and Judea to listen to Him. One day, as He was preaching to a great multitude, a palsied man was brought to Him but because of the crowd could not be carried into His presence. The carriers overcame this difficulty by loosening the tiles in the roof and lowering the sick man into a clear space in front of Christ. Christ said to the invalid,

Man, thy sins are forgiven thee. [Luke 5:20]

By claiming the power to forgive sins, He automatically claimed to be God. The Pharisees and doctors of the law immediately knew the import of these words and so began to comment on them, saying,

Who is this man who speaks blasphemies? Who can forgive sins, but God only? [Luke 5:21–22]

Christ retracted nothing. His answer to the Jews was pointed and tangible for He cured the palsied man of his ailment to prove that He had the power to forgive sins.

4. In the eighteenth and nineteenth chapters[4] of St. John's Gospel, there is an account which is significant in furthering the inquiry into the most important of Christ's claims.

In these chapters Christ was on trial before Pilate, the Roman procurator, because the Jewish courts lacked the jurisdiction to condemn a person to death. The trial was a public one and one in which the people played an important, though unofficial, part. During the trial, Pilate asked the crowd several questions concerning Christ and it is interesting to note how deftly the people's responses were directed by the chief priests and the Pharisees. In the responses to the questions of Pilate, the Jews never lost sight of their objective, which was to effect

4. John 18:28–40; John 19:1–16.

the death of Christ, and toward this end they gave Pilate two successive reasons for their demand.

Pilate thought that he could appease the rabble merely by scourging Jesus, but when he presented the scourged Christ to them, they demanded that He be crucified. Now the death penalty demanded a proportionately grave crime and so Pilate endeavored to find one. When he could not find one of his own for putting Christ to death, the Jews immediately presented him with theirs. It was,

We have a Law, and according to that Law he must die, because He made Himself Son of God. [John 19:7]

When Pilate perceived that it was on account of an alleged violation of a Jewish religious law and not on account of an imperial edict that the Jews had asked him to try and to condemn Christ, he showed himself disinterested in the whole affair and was for releasing Christ. When the Jews saw that their charge did not impress Pilate, they quickly changed it and presented him with one which was indeed designed to impress him and to force his hand to grant their wish. They accused Christ of being a rival to Caesar. Now, although the Romans permitted their subject peoples to keep their own local customs, religion and government, they ruthlessly put down rebellion. This was one of the chief tasks of the procurator. Knowing this, the Jews now urged the charge of rebellion against Christ, saying to Pilate:

If thou release this man, thou art no friend of Caesar; for everyone who makes himself king sets himself against Caesar. [John 19:7]

The sincerity of the Jews in bringing the charge of rebellion against Christ can be questioned. The Jews of this time were certainly not solicitous about preventing a rebellion in Caesar's empire. In fact, another reason why they sought the death of Christ was that He was not an anti-Roman, Jewish rebel. Josephus has written a history of the Jewish wars of rebellion against Rome which erupted after the death of Christ and which culminated in the destruction of Jerusalem in 70 A.D. From this, therefore, it can be seen that the charge of rebellion was not the real one which the Jews had in mind. This was but an expedient. The first charge was the real one, at least as far as the crowd was concerned, namely,

We have a Law, and according to that Law He must die, because He made Himself Son of God. [John 19:7]

Christ's initial silence before Pilate and the declarations which He finally did make are intelligible only if they are looked upon as a reaffirmation of the statements which caused the Jews to accuse Him of "pretending to be the Son of God."

5. Perhaps the classic passage for illuminating this topic is the twenty-sixth chapter of St. Matthew's Gospel. Herein is contained the account of Christ's trial before the Sanhedrin, a Jewish council qualified to try persons who had allegedly violated the religious law.

The first step in the procedure of the trial was to summon witnesses to testify. When two witnesses were found who agreed in their testimony, sentence was passed. But if the testimony of the witnesses was insufficient or indecisive, then the high priest, who was the head of the Sanhedrin, resorted to the formality of adjuration. Adjuration is the use of the name of God to confirm a command or a request. In this way, the Sanhedrin sought to discover the truth of the allegation. This legal process is perfectly exemplified[5] in the religious trial of Christ before the Sanhedrin.

From the moment that Christ was put on trial, the Sanhedrin sought to discover a crime which would not merely convict Him, but one which was serious enough to warrant the

5. Also see John 9:18–26.

death penalty. The Gospels report that it was unto this end that the chief priests called in false witnesses.

Now the chief priests and all the Sanhedrin were seeking false witness against Jesus, that they might put him to death, but they found none, though many false witnesses came forward. [Matt. 26:59]

When the first step in the trial failed to bring the hoped for result, the high priest took the second step which he knew would not fail. Since Christ had claimed divinity so many times in the past, the high priest had good reason to expect the same claim in answer to his adjuration. This would justify the death penalty. So the high priest stood up and said to Christ,

I adjure thee by the living God that thou tell us whether thou art the Christ, the Son of God. [Matt. 26:63]

Jesus answered,

Thou hast said it. Nevertheless, I say to you, hereafter you shall see the Son of Man sitting at the right hand of the Power[6] and coming upon the clouds of heaven. [Matt. 26:64]

At this the high priest tore his garments and said,

He has blasphemed; what further need have we of witnesses? Behold, now you have heard the blasphemy. What do you think? [Matt. 26:65]

They answered,

He is liable to death. [Matt. 26:66]

6. This phrase is an idiom which means that Christ is claiming equality with God in power.

From this account, it can be seen that the second part of the trial of Christ before the Sanhedrin worked out precisely as it had been planned by the chief priests and the elders of the Jews, but it is also a splendid proof that Christ claimed to be God.

Some investigators have said that Christ's claim to be the Son of God is to be taken in the figurative sense and not in the strictly literal sense. They say that even today a sailor is sometimes referred to as a "son of Neptune," and a soldier as a "son of Mars." Now there can be no doubt that in ancient times the Jewish people used the term "son of God" to describe figuratively a pious person. Did Christ refer to Himself as "the Son of God" in the figurative sense or in the strictly literal sense? Christ's parable of the tenants in the twentieth chapter[7] of St. Luke's Gospel answers this question and shows that Christ wished to be understood literally.

In the parable of the unjust tenants, there is a certain rich man who let out his vineyard to tenants and then went away for a long time. Upon his return, he sent his servants to collect his share of the fruits of the vineyard. But the tenants, instead of handing over the master's share to the servants, laid violent hands on them and wounded them. At length, the master sent his own son to collect his share of the fruits, thinking that surely the tenants would reverence him. But the tenants, when they saw the master's son coming, thought they could acquire the whole property if they did away with him. And so, laying violent hands on him, they slew him.

Christ did not even have to explain the parable to the chief priests and Pharisees who were listening to Him. While He was yet speaking, they knew whom the different characters of the parable represented. The master of the vineyard was God; the vineyard itself was Israel; the servants sent to collect the yield were the prophets; the unjust tenants were the leaders of the Jews; and the son of the master was Christ Himself. By the

7. Luke 20:9–20.

parable of the unjust tenants, Christ clearly shows that He does not refer to Himself as the Son of God in the loose, figurative sense, but He claims to be the Son of God in the strict, literal sense. He claims to be God because He claims equality with God.

The passages of the Gospels which have been examined in this chapter show that Christ claimed to be God. The first three passages deal with single instances where Christ claimed to be divine. But the passages which report the civil trial before Pilate and the religious trial before the Sanhedrin represent a great deal more than one or two instances of Christ's making this claim. Their tenor is that Christ had been making this assertion for a long time. The last passage examined repeats and explains the claim.

There is a uniform pattern in each of the passages discussed. Each passage has a three-fold probative force in showing that Christ claimed to be God. (1) In each passage, Christ's claim to divinity is explicit or clearly presumed. (2) In most of the passages, the Jews accused Christ of blasphemy for claiming to be divine and wished to inflict the punishment prescribed for blasphemers, for they remembered the decree of the Old Law, which read:

The man that curseth his God shall bear his sin. And he that blasphemeth the name of the Lord, dying let him die. All the multitude shall stone him.[8]

Those who made the charge of blasphemy certainly knew that for a man to claim to be God constituted blasphemy,[9] for in at least three of the passages, the persons who made the charges were Pharisees and doctors of the law. (3) In not one passage did Christ correct the Jews when they said that He claimed to

8. Leviticus 24:15–16.
9. Cf. also John 8:57–59.

be God. This is important for it shows that the Jews understood Him correctly, and, whenever Christ was misunderstood
by His listeners, He corrected their mistaken notions.[10] The
fact that in these passages Christ did not correct the Jews
showed that they understood Him as He wished to be understood. This strongly supports His original statements.

10. Matt. 16:5–12; Luke 22:35–38; John 4:30–35; John 6:32–36; John
8:21–24; John 8:31–38; John 11:11–16.

IX

Christ Appealed to His Miracles to Prove His Divinity

CHRIST WAS NOT CONTENT merely to claim to be God. To make unsupported claims leaves the door open to doubts and doubts eventually lead to disbelief. To prevent this state of affairs from developing, Christ matched His public claims with public proofs. He proved that He was God. The divine character of the deeds which He performed in support of His statements is clear and unmistakable. They show that He possessed the unbounded power that only God possesses.

It can be well be imagined with what comment the Jews received Christ's claim to be divine. In times past, others claimed to be the Messias but not in the clear-cut fashion in which Christ claimed to be not only the Messias but God Himself. The Jews saw only a man in Christ and so said that it was blasphemy for Him to claim to be God. This was the main reason for their disbelief in Him.

From the beginning of His public ministry, Christ is frequently portrayed in the Gospels as a teacher. He was not a teacher with a fixed place of instruction or a carefully selected group of students. It is true that Christ selected the Apostles and took special pains in teaching them; but it is also true that He was willing to teach anyone who was willing to listen to Him. He taught multitudes on the hillside, at the seashore, in the desert, in synagogues and within the precincts of the Temple.

In recording the fact that Christ taught under different circumstances, the Evangelists rarely omit the detail that when Christ was teaching or preaching He frequently used this opportunity to work miracles. The two activities usually went together. Although Christ could have taught even without working miracles, He generally did not. He linked the two as is clearly brought out by such passages as these:

And Jesus was going about all the towns and villages, teaching in their synagogues, and preaching the gospel of the kingdom, and curing every kind of disease and infirmity. [Matt. 9:35]

And when the Sabbath came, he began to teach in the synagogue. And many, when they heard him, were astonished at his doctrine, saying, "Where did he get all this?" and, "What mean such miracles wrought by his hands?" [Mark 6:1-2]

And coming down with them, he took his stand on a level stretch, with a crowd of his disciples, and a great multitude of people from all Judea and Jerusalem, and the sea coast of Tyre and Sidon, who came to listen to him and to be healed of their diseases. And those who were troubled with unclean spirits were cured. And all the crowd were trying to touch him, for power went forth from him and healed all. [Luke 6:18-19]

Now there was a certain man among the Pharisees, Nicodemus by name, a ruler of the Jews. This man came to Jesus at night, and said to him, "Rabbi, we know that thou hast come a teacher from God, for no one can work these signs that thou workest unless God be with him." [John 3:1-2]

The concurrence of miracles with instruction is too frequent and regular to be mere coincidence. One is strongly led to surmise that there is an intimate relationship between the two.

Investigation yields the reason why Christ worked miracles. They were worked to give added authority to His doctrines. The purpose of the miracles of Christ cannot be explained if one dissociates them from His teachings. Christ was not interested with merely impressing the people with His deeds. He did not care merely to inspire awe and wonderment. Christ rather wished the people to look upon His miracles as valid credentials and thereby be induced to accept His teaching. These passages bring out the bond between Christ's miracles and His doctrines:

Then Jesus answered and said to her, "O woman, great is thy faith. Let it be done to thee as thou wilt." And her daughter was healed from that moment. [Matt. 15:28]

And Jesus addressed him, saying, "What wouldst thou have me do for thee?" And the blind man said to him, "Rabboni, that I may see." And Jesus said to him, "Go thy way, thy faith has saved thee." And at once he received his sight. [Mark 10:51]

While he was yet speaking, there came one from the house of the ruler of the synagogue, saying to him, "Thy daughter is dead; do not trouble him." But Jesus on hearing this word, answered the father of the girl, "Do not be afraid; only have faith and she shall be saved." [Luke 8:49]

This first of his signs Jesus worked at Cana of Galilee; and he manifested his glory, and his disciples believed in him. [John 2:2]

These few selections prove that Christ worked miracles to lend cogency to His sayings. On some occasions, they were worked to dispose people to accept His doctrines; on others, they were worked to strengthen the faith of those who had already accepted them. Then too, it will be noticed that He refused to work miracles for those who, He saw, had already closed their minds to belief to Him.[1] The "faith" which Christ sought to instill in His followers was not merely a certain confidence in His powers. It was rather an intellectual assent to the doctrines which He was expounding. Christ's purpose, then, in working miracles was to drive home to His listeners the truth of His teachings.

An attentive reading of the Gospels reveals that the article of faith which Christ especially taught was that He was God. It is true He touched upon many doctrines which men must follow and believe to be saved, but the core of His teaching was His own divinity. Christ laid special stress on the doctrine that He was God because it was the cardinal point of His teachings. His other teachings receive their meaning from this one. This was to be the primary object of the faith of the people.

Christ worked miracles to lend added cogency to His teaching. But since Christ laid special emphasis on the doctrine of His divinity, it follows that the main reason for His working miracles was to prove His divinity. He explicitly stated that He worked miracles to prove that He was God:

"Go home to thy relatives, and tell them all that the Lord has done for thee." And he departed, and began to publish in Decapolis all that Jesus had done for him. And all marvelled. [Mark 5:19]

"The witness, however, that I have is greater than that of John. For the works which the Father has given me to accomplish, these very works that I do bear witness to me, that the Father has sent me." [John 5:36]

"If I do not perform the works of my Father, do not believe me. But if I do perform them, and if you are not willing to believe me, believe the works, that you may know and believe that the Father is in me and I in the Father." [John 10:38]

1. Luke 23:9.

"But the Father dwelling in me, it is he who does the works. Do you believe that I am in the Father and the Father in me? Otherwise believe because of the works themselves." [John 14:11]

Many other signs also Jesus worked in the sight of his disciples, which are not written in this book. But these are written that you may believe that Jesus is the Christ, the Son of God, and that believing you may have life in His name. [John 20:30]

How many miracles did Jesus Christ perform? It is impossible to determine the exact number with only the information which the Gospels contain. Felder counts thirty-five which are described in some detail:

1. Changing of the water into wine at Cana;
2. Healing of the ruler's son at Capharnaum;
3. Healing of the possessed at Capharnaum;
4. Healing of Peter's mother-in-law;
5. The first great catch of fishes;
6. Healing of a leper;
7. Healing of the paralytic at Capharnaum;
8. Healing at the pool at Bethsaida;
9. Healing of the withered hand;
10. Healing of the centurion's son;
11. Raising from the dead of the widow's son at Naim;
12. Healing of the blind men at Capharnaum;
13. Stilling the storm on the lake;
14. Healing of the possessed at Gerasa;
15. Healing of the woman with an issue of blood;
16. Raising from the dead of the daughter of Jairus;
17. Healing of the dumb possessed man;
18. Miraculous feeding of the five thousand;
19. Jesus walks on the Lake of Gennesaret;
20. Healing of the daughter of the Canaanite woman;
21. Healing of the deaf and dumb at Decapolis;
22. Miraculous feeding of the four thousand;

23. Healing of the blind man at Bethsaida;
24. Healing of the lunatic after the Transfiguration;
25. Catching of the fish with the coin in its mouth;
26. Healing of the man born blind;
27. Healing of the deaf and dumb possessed man;
28. Healing of the woman bowed over;
29. Healing of the dropsical man;
30. Raising from the dead of Lazarus;
31. Healing of the ten lepers;
32. Healing of the two men at Jericho;
33. Curse of the fig tree;
34. Healing of the ear of Malchus;
35. The second miraculous catch of fishes.[2]

It is certain that Christ worked a great many more miracles than are included in this particular list. The Evangelists group many miracles under such passages as:

And the blind and the lame came to him in the temple, and he healed them. [Matt. 21:14]

Now when it was evening, and the sun had set, they brought to him all who were ill and who were possessed. And the whole town had gathered together at the door. And he cured many who were afflicted with various diseases. [Mark 1:32–34]

In that very hour he cured many of diseases, and afflictions and evil spirits, and to many who were blind he granted sight. [Luke 7:21]

The chief priests and the Pharisees therefore gathered together a council, and said, "What are we doing? For this man is working many signs. If we let him alone as he is, all will believe in him." [John 11:47]

2. Felder, *Christ and the Critics*, trans. by Stoddard (London; Burns Oates and Washbourne, 1924), II, 281–82.

Not only were the miracles numerous, but they were of such a nature as to almost compel those who were benefited by them to reflect on their source and purpose. They were designed to influence man. Generally they were of an extremely personal nature. When Christ changed water to wine at Cana of Galilee, the miracle reached all of the guests at that wedding feast. When Christ stilled the storm on the Lake of Gennesaret, all the Apostles knew that it was their own lives that were saved and were forced to ask, "What kind of man is this who is obeyed even by the wind and by the sea?" When He preached to the five thousand in the desert, He chose to work a miracle which would affect each one of them individually. This characteristic of Christ's miracles fits in very neatly with His purpose in working them.

The conclusion to be drawn from this chapter is that Christ worked miracles to give added force to His doctrines, which was nothing less than God's own support of Christ's claims. By working miracles God Himself vouched for the truth of all that Christ taught. It is inconceivable that a miracle should confirm a false statement. This would mean that God approved a lie.

X

The Probative Force of the Miracles of Christ

IT IS HISTORICALLY certain that Christ claimed to be God and appealed to His works to prove His claim.[1] But are these works of such a character that they demand Uncreated Power for their performance? The importance of this question is apparent at once and for a satisfactory answer to it, the works of Christ must be investigated from the points of view of history, science and philosophy.

In a previous chapter it was shown that the Gospels are historically trustworthy documents and so the deeds which are attributed to Christ actually took place. Material science shows that these deeds are beyond the course of nature. Science deals with material, finite and proximate causes and effects and, although it has not discovered all the powers of nature, it certainly knows what is impossible for nature. Science then can only hint at the type of cause required to perform the deeds which Christ performed. If a work is of divine origin, it is clear that its cause must be infinite and ultimate. Now philosophy is the branch of learning which deals with ultimate causes. It is philosophy, not science, which can give a definite answer on the type of cause required to perform the deeds which Christ performed.

Rationalists deny that miracles have ever taken place on

1. Cf. Felder, *Christ and the Critics,* II, 240–61.

the score that they are impossible. They hold that the laws of nature are absolutely unchangeable by either God or man and so do not admit of any alteration or suspension. Miracles, they say, violate the laws of nature. For this reason, critics affirm that Christ's miracles are either empty fabrications or capable of natural explanation.

There is error in the reasoning of the rationalists and the root of this error is that they hold that the laws of nature are absolutely immutable. We cannot admit that God is powerless to change or suspend the workings of the laws of nature. These laws do not exist independently of the created things they govern. They cannot be dissociated from something which moves. Without things to be governed there would be no laws of nature.

While examining the proofs for the existence of God, we say that all creatures are beings absolutely dependent on God for existence and preservation. They are contingent beings and cannot be otherwise. The laws of nature are contingent on the existence of created things and created things are contingent on God who can, therefore, manipulate the laws of nature in any way that He sees fit. He can certainly suspend the operation of a law in any given instance. And this is precisely what a miracle is. It is the suspension of a law of nature and not its destruction or violation as critics falsely think it is. *A miracle which is of value in apologetics is defined as a sensible act exceeding the manner of acting of all created natures and so is producible only by God and is wrought to attest the divine origin of revelation.*

A miracle might exceed the laws of nature in one of three ways.

a. It is a miracle to produce something which is never found in nature as, for example, the earth standing still or two objects occupying the same place.

b. It is a miracle to produce something found in nature but never found in this object in nature. The ability to see is found in nature but only a miracle can give sight to one congenitally blind.

c. An effect which might be produced naturally can be produced miraculously. For example, it would be a miracle if the cure of an ailment which might be effected by medicine or rest were brought about instantaneously.

The object of this chapter is to show that the miracles of Christ are acts which require the power that God possesses and as such prove the divine authorization of His mission. They are God's seal guaranteeing the truth of Christ's doctrines and the validity of His jurisdiction.

1. The first type of miracles which require divine power are miracles of creation. Creation is the bringing into actual existence a being which previously had only possible existence. It is not used here in its loose sense when it might mean the production of the unusual or the novel; nor does it mean to reshape or refashion already existing material. We now show that to create requires the infinite power which belongs only to God and which cannot be communicated to others.

A. Every created being whether it be of the material or the spiritual order is the effect of a higher cause. It has a received or a contingent existence. If we took all created things in existence as a unit, we would have the most universal effect. This universal effect could have been brought into existence only by the action of the most universal cause which by very definition has unlimited or infinite power and is called God.

B. The production of a thing simply means that a cause brings about an effect. Now if this effect has already been partially produced, then less power is required to complete it than would be required to produce it entirely. Less is required to remodel a house than is required to build it new; the revision of a book is easier than the original writing. In these instances there is something to start with and therefore less to supply. In other words, the more actual an effect already is, the less power will be demanded of the cause. But the converse of this is also true, namely, the less actual a thing is, the more power will be demanded of the cause to complete the effect.

A thing that is to be created has absolutely no actual existence or perfection before the cause begins to operate. It is in the realm of pure possibility. Since it can in no way lessen the power required of the cause, that cause must be the direct opposite of that which is pure potentiality. It must then be pure actuality or perfection. God alone is Pure Perfection and so He alone can create.

The proof that only God can create may be stated more graphically in this fashion. The "gulf" or "distance" between this stone which I hold in my hand and a non-existing stone is measureless or infinite. The reason for this is plain. For an interval or gulf to be measurable, it must be bound by two definite terminals. But the "distance" between an existing stone and a non-existing stone is not bounded by two definite terminals and therefore cannot be measured. It is measureless or infinite. To bridge the measureless or infinite gulf between nothingness and somethingness requires correspondingly measureless or infinite power which only God has. God alone, therefore, can bring something into existence out of nothing or create.

With the requisite conditions for creation firmly in mind, one examines two passages from the Gospels:

His disciples came to him saying, "This is a desert place and the hour is already late; send the crowds away, so that they may go into the villages and buy themselves food." But Jesus said to them, "They do not need to go away; you yourselves give them some food." They answered him, "We have here only five loaves and two fishes." He said to them, "Bring them here to me." And when he had ordered the crowd to recline on the grass, he took the five loaves and two fishes, and looking up to heaven, blessed and broke the loaves and gave them to his disciples, and the disciples gave them to the crowds. And all ate and were satisfied; and they gathered up what was left over, twelve baskets full of fragments. Now the number of those who had eaten was five thousand men, without counting women and children. [Matt. 14:15-21]

In those days when again there was a great crowd, and they had nothing to eat, he called his disciples together and said to them, "I have compassion on the crowd, for behold, they have been with me three days, and have nothing to eat; and if I send them away to their homes fasting, they will faint on the way, for some of them have come from a distance." And his disciples answered him, "How will anyone be able to satisfy these with bread, here in the desert?" And he asked them, "How many loaves have you?" And they said, "Seven." And he bade the crowd to recline on the ground. Then taking the seven loaves, he gave thanks, broke them and gave them to his disciples to distribute. And they had a few little fishes; and he blessed them, and ordered them to be distributed. And all ate and were satisfied; and they took up what was left of the fragments, seven baskets. Now those who had eaten were about four thousand. [Mark 8:1-9]

Notice how on each of these two occasions Christ sets the stage to throw these actions into bold and unmistakable relief. The people have no bread with them when they begin to listen to Christ. He draws them into the desert where there is no bread and where food cannot be procured in time to feed large multitudes. In these circumstances He performs works which force each and every one of the over four and five thousand persons to attribute his relief from hunger to Christ. In the first instance, five loaves and two fishes are presented to Christ; in the second, there are seven loaves and a few fishes. Christ multiplied them so that after the multitudes had eaten well, twelve baskets of fragments were gathered up from the scene of the first miracle and seven hampers from the second. On each of these occasions, Christ worked at least one miracle. But it is possible that He did not create all the bread to feed the multitudes at one time. He may have created new amounts of it as it was distributed. This would indicate that Christ worked a series of miracles on each of these occasions. Commentators are not decided as to whether or not the miracles of the multiplication of the loaves and fishes were miracles of creation or of immediate substantial change. In either case their probative force is the same for in both cases they could have been worked only by the power of God.

2. There is another kind of act which requires the power that only God possesses. It is called immediate substantial change. Only God can so completely and immediately change the nature of a thing so that where it once exhibited one set of properties, it now exhibits an entirely new set.

A. To be able to effect immediate substantial change requires the power to create which we have already seen only God possesses. It was shown that only God as the universal cause can bring about the universal effect called being. Now in the substantial change of which we speak, the power which acts must be able to reach the inner nature of a thing, that is, its very being. It is not enough to modify externals as a carpenter modifies the shape of wood for this wood obviously still exhibits the same set of properties as before thus proving that its substance was not changed. Since only God can create, He alone has absolute and immediate control over the very being of a thing and so He alone can change its inner nature.

B. In the instances already examined, we saw that only God can lift a thing out of the realm of possibility into the realm of actuality. The only being that can create is the one that can bring about an effect without any intermediary or instrument. We now show that God alone can change the substance of one thing into that of another because He alone can act without an intermediary.

The ultimate components of every material thing are the two incomplete principles of matter known as prime matter and substantial form. These two incomplete principles cannot exist independently of each other. Where one is present, the other must be present. They are not like the atoms of hydrogen and oxygen which combine to form molecules of water. These atoms can have independent existence and are the proximate components of matter. Prime matter and substantial form do not have independent existence and are the ultimate components of matter.

Prime matter gives a thing its bulk or mass. It is the same in every object and so we cannot say that it is because of prime matter that one thing has a nature different from another thing. When we consider it by itself, it is undetermined. It does not possess a specific set of properties, but it is the substratum of all substantial change. Substantial form is the principle which makes one thing different from another. It determines prime matter so that the resultant object has its own special nature. It gives a thing a specific set of properties. For example, in the assimilation of food, substance which was non-living is now living. In this change, the prime matter remained the same but the substantial form was changed since different sets of properties were exhibited.

Where substantial form determines prime matter, the result is a single complete material object. It is a unity, but unity implies that the two principles are joined immediately, that is, without the mediation of a third principle which holds them together. If matter and form were joined mediately, the result would not be a unity but several unities bound together.

Since prime matter and substantial form are joined immediately, it is only the Being that can act immediately, that can change the substantial form of an object without the use of intermediaries. Agents with limited power such as angels, men, or devils cannot create because they cannot act immediately and so cannot effect an immediate change of substantial form; they cannot change substances with the use of instruments.

Inorganic matter, plants, animals and man are essentially different things. They have different sets of properties which indicate the presence of different substantial forms. To bring the dead back to life, to change water into wine, to cure the congenitally blind implies the power to act immediately—a power which only God possesses.

Everything must act according to its nature—a stone must act like a stone, an animal like an animal and so forth. All creatures have fixed and limited natures and so cannot work a miracle which by very definition exceeds the manner of acting of all created nature and possible only for the unlimited power of God. It is clear, then, that the objections which hold that miracles could have been worked by yet undiscovered powers in nature are groundless.

There are several episodes in the Gospels which must be evaluated in the light of the philosophical explanation just concluded:

Martha, the sister of him who was dead, said to him, "Lord, by this time he is already decayed, for he is dead four days." And Jesus, raising his eyes, said, "Father, I give thee thanks." When he had said this, he cried out with a loud voice, "Lazarus, come forth." And at once he who had been dead came forth, bound feet and hands with bandages, and his face tied up with a cloth. Jesus said to them, "Unbind him, and let him go." [John 12:1]

And it came to pass afterwards, that he went to a town called Naim. And as he drew near the gate of the town, behold, a dead man was being carried out. And he went up and touched the stretcher. And he said, "Young man, I say to thee, arise." And he who was dead, sat up, and began to speak. [Luke 7:11–16]

There came one from the house of the ruler of the synagogue, saying to him, "Thy daughter is dead." But Jesus answered the father of the girl, "Do not be afraid." And when he came to the house all were weeping for her. But he said, "Do not weep; she is asleep, not dead." And they laughed him to scorn, knowing that she was dead. But he taking her by the hand, cried out, saying, "Girl, arise." And her spirit returned, and she rose up immediately. [Luke 8:49-55]

But when John had heard in prison of the works of Christ, he sent two of his disciples to say to him, "Art thou he who is come, or shall we look for another?" And Jesus answering said to them, "Go and report to John what you have heard and seen: the blind see, the lame walk, the lepers are cleansed, the deaf hear, the dead arise." [Matt. 11:2-5]

In each of these selected instances there is a substantial change. A dead body exhibits an essentially different set of properties from a living body; and water is essentially different from wine. This indicates that the substantial forms are different. In the Gospel accounts it is Christ who immediately brings about the change. When it is borne in mind that immediate substantial change requires Uncreated or Divine Power, it will clearly be seen that these miracles prove that Jesus Christ is God.

The most important miracle of immediate substantial change in proof of His divinity is Christ's resurrection from the dead. This miracle is examined separately, not because its probative force is different from the other instances of resurrection, but because its actuality has been bitterly contested by investigators of the rationalistic persuasion. The objections of these authors revolve about the theme that Christ was not really dead when He was buried: that, in the tomb, He recovered His powers and health; and that three days later He presented Himself to the world as One Who had come back from the dead. But do the Gospels support this theory? These are some of the passages from the Gospel which throw light on the question of the actuality of Christ's death:

But when they came to Jesus, and saw that he was already dead, they did not break his legs; but one of the soldiers opened his side with a lance, and immediately there came out blood and water. [John 19:32–34]

Joseph of Arimathea went in boldly to Pilate and asked for the body of Jesus. But Pilate wondered whether he had already died. And sending for the centurion, he asked whether he was already dead. And when he learned from the centurion that he was, he granted the body to Joseph. [Mark 15:43–46]

The chief priests and the Pharisees went in a body to Pilate, saying, "Sir, we have remembered how that deceiver said, *while he was yet alive,* 'After three days I will rise again.' " [Matt. 28:63]

If the death of Christ was but an apparent death, the rationalists must quote their sources for holding this. Let them not appeal to the Gospels for support of their theory, for the Gospels do not leave even a vestige of a doubt that Christ really died.

The task of bringing out the force of this miracle is completed by showing that Christ really arose from the dead. These are the passages pertinent to this question:

Now when he had risen from the dead early on the first day of the week, he appeared first to Mary Magdalene, out of whom he had driven seven devils. She went and took word to those who had been with him. And they, hearing that he was alive and had been seen by her, did not believe it. [Mark 16:9–12]

And rising up that very hour, they returned to Jerusalem, where they found the Eleven gathered together and those who were with them, saying, "The Lord has risen indeed, and has appeared to Simon." [Luke 24:33–35]

After this he was manifested in another form to two of them, as they were on their way into the country. And they went and took word to the rest, and even then they did not believe. [Mark 16:12-13]

Now Thomas, one of the Twelve, called the Twin, was not with them when Jesus came. The other disciples therefore said to him, "We have seen the Lord." But he said to them, "Unless I see in his hands the print of the nails, and put my finger into the place of the nails, and put my hand into his side, I will not believe." And after eight days, his disciples were again inside, and Thomas with them, Jesus came and said, "Peace be to you." Then he said to Thomas, "Bring here thy finger, and see my hands; and bring here thy hand, and put it into my side; and do not be unbelieving, but believing." Thomas said to him, "My Lord and my God." [John 20:24-28]

Now while they were going, behold, some of the guards came into the city and reported to the chief priest all that had happened. And when they had assembled with the elders, and had consulted together they gave much money to the soldiers, telling them, "Say, 'His disciples came by and stole him while we were sleeping.' And if the procurator hears of this, we will persuade him and keep you out of trouble." And they took the money, and did as they were instructed; and this story has been spread abroad among the Jews even to the present day. [Matt. 28:11-15]

The passages which have been taken from the Gospels in connection with the resurrection of Christ are not merely a collection of texts which prove the same fact, namely that Christ really arose from the dead, but also they include the details which answer the principal objections and counter-explanations of the rationalists against the actuality of Christ's resurrection.

a. The evidence which is brought forth to prove the resurrection of Christ is not merely negative, such as the fact that the tomb was empty; but the evidence is also positive for it shows that Christ appeared to the people on eight different occasions.

b. It reveals that the story of the stolen body was an expedient fabrication on the part of the leaders of the people.

c. The fact that Christ invited the Apostles to touch Him and that He ate with them proves that Christ did not possess a phantom body, as certain ancient writers said He did.[2]

d. The Apostles were not easily-led persons, but rather, they were slow to believe.

e. The Gospel accounts show that the Apostles were not the victims of hallucinations. The persons to whom Christ appeared after His resurrection were too numerous, too incredulous, and too much in agreement for their experiences to be explained as hallucinations.

3. There is a third category of phenomena which can be produced only by God. These are the effects which are morally miraculous. By this we mean that the emphasis is not on "what is produced" as was the case in miracles of creation and substantial change but rather on "how the effect is produced." We shall see that the manner in which a thing is made might be possible only to God.

In the world about us there are many instances of chemical reactions whereby one substance is transformed into another one. Lifeless food or even inorganic material becomes living flesh; water becomes wine through the process of fermentation. But notice that in each of these instances the transformation took place according to fixed and definite laws implanted in these materials. The change came about gradually. There was a period in which the "raw material" was prepared to be converted into the new substance. Experience tells us that as far as nature is concerned the operation of those laws which accompany the change might be speeded up but it can never be dispensed with.

The laws of nature which operate to bring about change are not found in isolation. They are in force everywhere for

2. Tixeront, *History of Dogmas,* 3rd edition (St. Louis; Herder Book Co., 1930), I, 133B.

they know no barrier of time and place. But these laws are contingent and not absolute and so they owe their existence to the Author of nature Who is God. It is entirely in keeping with common sense that only God Who made the law can dispense from its operation in a particular instance. This is precisely what takes place when a natural phenomenon is produced miraculously. God alone can bring about an effect without the operation of the laws that ordinarily bring it about. Most of Christ's miracles are of this third category. We include the accounts of but a few of them here.

And on the third day a wedding took place at Cana of Galilee. Jesus too was invited. And the wine having run short, the mother of Jesus said to him, "They have no wine." . . . Jesus said to them, "Fill the jars with water."

And they filled them to the brim. And Jesus said to them, "Draw out now, and take it to the chief steward." When the chief steward had tasted the water after it had become wine, not knowing whence it was (though the attendants who had drawn the water knew) called the bridegroom. . . . This first of his signs Jesus worked at Cana of Galilee and he manifested his glory. [John 2:7–11]

When he said these things, he spat on the ground and made clay with the spittle, and spread the clay over his eyes, and said to him, "Go, wash in the pool of Siloe. . . ." So he went away, and washed and returned seeing. [John 9:6–7]

And as he was entering a certain village, there met him ten lepers, who stood afar off and lifted up their voice, crying, "Jesus, master, have pity on us." And when he saw them, he said, "Go show thyselves to the priests." And it came to pass as they were on their way, that they were made clean. But one of them, seeing that he was made clean, returned, with a loud voice glorifying God, and he fell

THE PROBATIVE FORCE OF MIRACLES

on his face at his feet, giving thanks; and he was a Samaritan.
[Luke 17:12–16]

And behold, there was a certain man before him who had the
dropsy. And Jesus asked the lawyers and Pharisees, saying, "Is it
lawful to cure on the Sabbath?" But they remained silent. And he
took and healed him and let him go. [Luke 14:2–4]

The miracles discussed are not the only ones which have
probative force. These particular ones were selected because
in the opinion of the author their cogency can more easily be
brought out. All true apologetical miracles must be traced to
God as their author. They are God's stamp of approval on the
teachings of the wonderworker. Miracles are a divine proof of
the truth of all of Christ's doctrines, and specifically of His
statement that He is God.

XI

The Prophecies of Christ

THE ABILITY to work miracles was not the only unusual power that Christ had. He also made predictions. The predictions which He made were out of the ordinary and so are worthy of study. They are called prophecies and are important because they throw additional light upon the already clear identity of Christ.

The word "prophecy" has been used very loosely in both ancient and modern literature, and has thus acquired a variety of meanings. This makes it imperative that its meaning in this discussion be precisely defined. As it is used here, a prophecy is defined as a detailed and certain prediction of a definite future event, the foretelling of which is impossible by natural prevision or guess because the event predicted depends on many free causes for its fulfillment. By this definition, correct guesses or predictions made after a study of the possible concurrent causes are not prophecies; nor can one label as prophecies those ambiguous statements which could be fulfilled by the concurrence of a variety of events such as were the statements given out by the ancient pagan oracles.

For a prophecy to have any value in apologetics, it must already have been fulfilled. It is after the details of a prophecy have taken place that unaided reason will stamp it as a prediction made without guess or prevision and will inquire into the type of intelligence which could have made this prophecy.

Attentive reading of the Gospels shows that Christ made

certain statements which He intended to be understood as predictions of future events. These statements must be examined to determine whether or not they are detailed enough to be true prophecies. Historical documents must be searched to determine whether or not these predictions have come to pass.

The prophecies of Christ which have apologetic value can be broken down into four categories, namely, those which deal with Christ Himself, those which deal with persons close to Christ, those which deal with the destruction of Jerusalem, and those which deal with Christ's followers in future ages.

1. Christ's predictions concerning Himself deal with events which were to accompany His passion and death:

But while all were marvelling at all the things that he was doing, he said to his disciples, "Store up these words in your minds; the Son of Man is to be betrayed into the hands of men." [Luke 9:45]

Now while they were gathering in Galilee, Jesus said to them, "The Son of Man is to be betrayed into the hands of men, and they will kill him; and on the third day he will rise again." [Matt. 16:21]

And it came to pass when Jesus had finished all these words, that he came to his disciples, "You know that after two days the Passover will be here; and the Son of Man will be delivered up to be crucified." [Matt. 26:1–2]

And as Jesus was going up to Jerusalem, he took the twelve disciples aside by themselves, and said to them, "Behold, we are going up to Jerusalem, and the Son of Man will be betrayed to the chief priests and the Scribes; and they will condemn him to death, and will deliver him to the Gentiles to be mocked and scourged and crucified; and on the third day he will rise again." [Matt. 20:17–20]

A considerable number of details are included in these four predictions of Christ. They are sufficiently detailed and definite to exclude the possibility of guess or prevision, for Christ specifies the time, place, circumstance of arrest, and the manner of death.

In fulfillment of these prophecies, the Gospels show that it was at the Paschal time[1] that Christ was put to death.

The Jews therefore, since it was the Preparation Day, in order that the bodies might not remain upon the cross on the Sabbath . . . besought Pilate that their legs might be broken. [John 19:31]

Now in the place where he was crucified there was a garden, and in the garden a new tomb in which no one had yet been laid. There, accordingly, because of the Preparation Day of the Jews, for the tomb was close at hand, they laid Jesus. [John 19:41]

The Gospels imply that the place of Christ's condemnation and death was the city of Jerusalem. Olivet, Gethsemane and Calvary were proper places near Jerusalem. Then, too, it must be noticed that Christ was tried before the Jewish Sanhedrin which convened in Jerusalem. A third reason for saying that Christ suffered and died at Jerusalem was the fact that Pilate was there at that time. Ordinarily the Roman procurators resided at Caesarea on the coast, but at every Paschal season they took a detachment of soldiers with them and went to Jerusalem to guard against a possible Jewish insurrection. This accounts for the fact that Pilate happened to be in Jerusalem when Christ died.

The Gospels show that Christ was mocked before He died:

And they answered and said, "He is liable to death." Then they spat in his face and buffeted him; while others struck his face with the palms of their hands, saying, "Prophecy to us, O Christ, who is it that struck thee." [Matt. 26:67]

Then the soldiers of the procurator took Jesus into the praetorium, and gathered together about him the whole cohort. And they

1. Cf. also Matt. 27:62.

stripped him and put on him a scarlet cloak; and plaiting a crown of thorns, they put it on his head, and a reed into his right hand; and bending the knee before him they mocked him, saying, "Hail, King of the Jews." And they spat on him, and took the reed and kept striking him on the head. And when they had mocked him, they took the cloak off him and put on his own garments, and led him away to crucify him. [Matt. 27:27-31]

There is clear evidence that Christ died by crucifixion:

Now there were also two other malefactors led to execution with him. And when they came to the place, the Skull, they crucified him there, and the robbers, one on his right hand and the other on his left. [Luke 23:32]

This group of prophecies of Christ concerning Himself is concluded by pointing out that Christ foretold that He would arise from the dead.

In answer Jesus said to them, "Destroy this temple, and in three days I will raise it up." The Jews therefore said, "Forty-six years has this temple been in building, and wilt thou raise it up in three days?" But he was speaking of the temple of his body. When accordingly, he had risen from the dead, his disciples remembered that he had said this. [John 2:19]

The Gospels which contain the prophecies of Christ are themselves the historical documents which prove that they were fulfilled.

2. The second category of Christ's prophecies includes those prophecies made concerning persons who were close to Him. These persons were Peter, Judas and Mary Magdalene.

A. In a detailed fashion Christ foretold that Peter would deny Him. On the occasion of the Last Supper, Christ said to the Apostles,

"You will all be scandalized this night because of me: for it is written, 'I will smite the shepherd and the sheep of the flock will be scattered.' " . . . But Peter answered and said to him, "Even though all shall be scandalized because of thee, I will never be scandalized." Jesus said to him, "Amen I say to thee, this very night, before the cock crows, thou wilt deny me thrice." [Matt. 26:31]

Notice how the Evangelist includes in this passage a detail which precludes the possibility of Christ's having natural prevision. He pictures Peter and the other Apostles vehement in professing their allegiance to Christ.

St. Matthew's Gospel contains the account of the fulfillment of Christ's prophecy of Peter's denial.

Now Peter was sitting outside in the courtyard; and a maidservant came up to him and said, "Thou also wast with Jesus the Galilean." But he denied it before them all, saying, "I do not know what thou art saying." And when he had gone out to the gateway, another maid saw him, and said to those who were there, "This man also was with Jesus of Nazareth." And again he denied with an oath, "I do not know the man." And after a little while the bystanders came up and said to Peter, "Surely thou also art one of them, for even thy speech betrays thee." Then he began to curse and to swear that he did not know the man. And at that moment the cock crowed. And Peter remembered the word that Jesus had said, "Before a cock crows, thou wilt deny me thrice." And he went out and wept bitterly. [Matt. 26:69-75]

B. Christ predicted that Judas would betray Him.

And while they were eating, he said, "Amen I say to you, one of you will betray me." And being very much saddened they began each to say, "Is it I, Lord?" But he answered and said, "He who dips his hand with me in the dish, he will betray me. . . . it is better for that man if he had not been born." And Judas who betrayed him answered and said, "Is it I, Rabbi?" He said to him, "Thou hast said it." [Matt. 26:21-25]

The following passages show that Christ's prediction concerning His betrayal by Judas came to pass.

"Sleep on now, and take your rest. Behold the hour is at hand, and the Son of Man will be betrayed into the hands of sinners. Rise, let us go. Behold, he who betrays me is at hand." And while he was yet speaking, behold Judas, one of the Twelve, came and with him a great crowd with swords and clubs, from the chief priests and elders of the people. Now his betrayer had given them a sign, saying, "Whomever I kiss, that is he, lay hold of him." And he went straight up to Jesus and said, "Hail, Rabbi," and kissed him. And Jesus said to him, "Friend, for what purpose hast thou come?" Then they came forward and set hands on Jesus and took him. [Matt. 26:45]

C. Christ prophecied that the fact that His Body was annointed by Mary Magdalene would become universally known. This prophecy is brief but the amount of detail that it contains makes it impossible for it to have been made by guess or prevision. It has great apologetic value.

Now when Jesus was in Bethany, in the house of Simon the leper, a woman came up to him with an alabaster jar of precious ointment, and she poured it on his head, as he reclined at table. But when the disciples saw this, they were indignant. . . . Jesus, perceiving it, said to them, "Why do you trouble the woman? She has done me a good turn . . . she has done it for my burial. Amen I say to you, wherever in the whole world this gospel is preached, this also that she has done shall be told in memory of her." [Matt. 26:6–13]

The fact that the story of the anointing of Christ's body by Mary is included in all the integral manuscripts of the Gospels, either in the original language or in translations in all countries since the time of the Apostles, is proof that this prophecy has been fulfilled.

3. Christ predicted the destruction of the city of Jerusalem. He couched it in such detail that there can be no doubt that He was referring to a definite event.

And when he drew near and saw the city, he wept over it saying, "If thou hadst known, in this thy day, even thou the things that are for thy peace. But now they are hidden from thy eyes. For the days will come upon thee when thy enemies will throw up a rampart about thee, and surround thee and shut thee in on every side, and will dash thee to the ground and thy children within thee, and will not leave in thee one stone upon another." [Luke 19:41-44]

"And when you see Jerusalem being surrounded by an army, then know that her desolation is at hand. . . . For there will be great distress over the land, and wrath upon this people. And they will fall by the edge of the sword, and will be led away as captives to all the nations. And Jerusalem will be trodden down by the Gentiles." [Luke 21:20-23]

And as he was going out of the temple, one of his disciples said to him, "Master, look, what wonderful stones and buildings." And Jesus answered and said to him, "Dost thou see all these great buildings? There will not be left one stone upon another that will not be thrown down." [Mark 13:1-3]

Although the Jewish writer, Josephus (c. 37–95 A.D.) has written a great deal on this subject, space permits only the inclusion of certain passages which touch upon the prophecy of Christ. The entire account can be read in his writing entitled *The Jewish Wars*. These are the passages which touch upon the prophecy of Christ:

The whole empire being now secured and the Roman state saved beyond expectation, Vespasian turned his thoughts to what remained in Judea. He was, however, anxious himself to take ship for Rome as soon as the winter was over and was rapidly settling affairs in Alexandria; but he dispatched his son Titus with picked forces to crush Jerusalem.[2]

Titus then withdrew to Antonia,[3] determined on the following day, at dawn, to attack with his whole force and invest the temple. That building, however, God indeed long since had sentenced to the flames; but now in the revolution of the years had arrived the fated day, the tenth of the month of Lous,[4] the day on which of old it had been burned by the king of Babylon. The flames, however, owed their origin and cause to God's own people. For on the withdrawal of Titus, the insurgents, after a brief respite, again attacked the Romans, and an engagement ensued between the guards of the sanctuary and the troops who were endeavouring to extinguish the fire in the inner court . . . At this moment, one of the soldiers, awaiting no orders and with no horror of so dread a deed, but moved by some supernatural impulse, snatched a brand from the burning timber and, hoisted up by one of his comrades, flung the fiery missile through the low golden floor, which gave access on the north side to the chambers surrounding the sanctuary.[5]

The Romans, now masters of the walls, planted their standards on the towers, and with clapping of hands and jubilation raised a paeon in honor of their victory. They found the end of the war a much lighter task than the beginning; indeed, they could hardly believe that they had surmounted the last wall without bloodshed, and, seeing none to oppose them were truly perplexed. Pouring into the alleys, sword in hand, they massacred indiscriminately all whom they met, and burned the houses with all who had taken refuge within. Often in the course of the raids, on entering the houses for loot, they found whole families dead and rooms filled with the victims of the famine, and then, shuddering at the sight, retired empty handed. Yet, while they pitied those who had thus perished, they had no similar feelings for the living, but,

2. *Jewish Wars*, trans. by H. St. J. Thackeray and Ralph Marcus, "Loeb Classical Library" (London; Heinemann, 1928), Bk. IV, 657. Used with permission of Harvard University Press.

3. This was the name of a fortress adjoining the temple.

4. This is the month of August in the Macedonian calendar.

5. *Jewish Wars* Bk. VI. 50–53.

running everyone through who fell in their way, they choked the alleys with corpses and deluged the whole city with blood, insomuch that many fires were extinguished by the gory stream. Toward evening they ceased slaughtering, but when night fell, the fire gained mastery, and the dawn of the eighth day of the month of Gorpiaeus[6] broke upon Jerusalem in flames—a city which had suffered such calamities during the seige. . . .

Titus, on entering the city, was amazed at its strength. . . . And when, at a later period, he demolished the rest of the city and raised the walls, he left these towers as a memorial of his attendant fortune.[7]

It was in circumstances such as Josephus describes that Christ's prophecy concerning the destruction of Jerusalem came to pass.

4. At various times during His public ministry, Christ predicted what would befall His followers because of their loyalty to Him. The predictions are detailed and definite enough to rule out ambiguity. Christ said:

"But before all these things they will arrest you and persecute you, delivering you up to the synagogues and prisons, dragging you before kings and governors for my name's sake. It shall lead to your bearing witness." [Luke 31:12][8]

There is abundant evidence in ancient literature that the prediction of Christ concerning the fate of many of His followers has been fulfilled. One of the earliest references to the persecutions directed against the followers of Christ is found in a writing of the pagan Latin writer Tacitus:

Therefore, to scotch the rumour, Nero substituted as culprits and punished with the utmost refinements of cruelty, a class of men,

6. This is the month of September in the Macedonian calendar.
7. *Jewish Wars* Bk. VI. 403–413.
8. Cf. also Matt. 10:17–23.

PROPHECIES OF CHRIST

PROPHECIES OF CHRIST FULFILMENT (arranged as a diagram)

Left column (Prophecies)

1. Prophecies concerning Self
a—He would be mocked and scourged.
(Mt. XX-17/20)

b—He would die by crucifixion. (Matt. XXVI-1/2)

c—He would rise from the dead. (Matt. XVI-21)

2. Prophecies concerning persons near to Him
a—He would be denied by Peter. (Matt. XXVI-31/35)

b—He would be betrayed by Judas.
(Matt. XXVI-21/25)

c—His anointing by Mary Magdalene would be told universally. (Matt. XXVI-6/13)

3. Prophecies concerning the destruction of the city of Jerusalem.
a—Jerusalem would be beseiged. (Lk. XIX-41/44)

b—The people living in Jerusalem would be massacred during the siege. (Lk. XXI-20/23)

c—The Temple at Jerusalem would be destroyed.
(Mk. XIII-1/3)

4. Prophecies concerning His followers and Church.
a—Christians of all ages and age levels would be persecuted, imprisoned and put to death for being followers of Christ. (Jn. XV-18; Jn. XVI-1)

b—The Gospel would be preached and the Church would be spread among all nations. (Lk. XXIV-46)

Right column (Fulfilment)

1. Fulfilment of Prophecies concerning Self
a—He was mocked as king of Jews. (Matt. XXVII-27)

b—Christ died by crucifixion.
(Lk. XXIII-32 & Tacitus, Annales. XV. 44)

c—Christ arose from the dead. (Jn. II-19/22)

2. Fulfilment of prophecies concerning persons near to Christ.
a—Peter denied Christ when he had been seized.
(Matt. XXVI-69/75)

b—Judas betrayed Christ in the Garden of Gethsemane. (Matt. XXVI-45/50)

c—The account of Mary Magdalene's kindness has been diffused, for all integral Mss. of the New Testament contain it.

3. Fulfilment of the prophecies of the destruction of the city of Jerusalem.
a—Jerusalem was besieged by the Roman armies under Titus in 70 A.D. (Jewish Wars—VI-403ff)

b—Jerusalem's population was massacred during the Roman seige. (Jewish Wars—VI-403)

c—Jerusalem's Temple was destroyed in the Roman invasion and seige. (Jewish Wars—VI-50ff)

4. Fulfilment of prophecies concerning Christ's followers and the Church.
a—Christians have always suffered for being followers of Christ. (Tacitus, Annales. XV. 44; Tertullian in Apologeticum; Allard Ten Lectures on Martyrs. Cf. pp. 168ff)

b—The Church and Gospel are universally diffused.
(cf. pp. 140ff)

loathed for their vices, styled Christians . . . First, then, the confessed members of the sect were arrested; next, on their disclosures, vast numbers were convicted, not so much on the count of arson as for hatred of the human race. And derision accompanied their end; they were covered with wild beasts' skins and torn to death by dogs; or they were fastened on crosses, and when daylight failed, were burned to serve as lamps by night.[9]

There are scores of texts in the writings of the ancient Christian writers[10] which prove the fact that Christ's followers were persecuted for His sake.

The predictions of Christ which have been examined in these pages are prophecies of apologetic value. In each case the prophecy itself has been detailed and definite and free from ambiguity. The accounts of their fulfillment are clear and unmistakable.

The student will acquire a deeper insight into the purpose of Christ's prophecies as soon as he realizes the period of time in which they were fulfilled. Their fulfillment was so spaced that their force was driven home to widening groups of persons. The first two groups of Christ's prophecies came to pass at the time of Christ's passion and death and so were designed to influence the Apostles and some of the Jews. The second group of prophecies forced its attention on a much greater number of people, namely, all the Jews of Palestine as well as the visitors from the Diaspora,[11] who were trapped in Jerusalem at the time of its destruction. The last category of prophecies will force their attention upon the people of every age for in all ages Christ's followers will be persecuted.

9. Tacitus, *Annales* Bk. XV, 44, trans. by John Jackson in Loeb Classical Library (London; Heinemann, 1937).

10. Read Allard, *Ten Lectures on the Martyrs,* trans. by Cappadelta, 2nd Edition (New York; Benziger, 1907).

11. By "Diaspora" is meant the Jews who lived outside of Palestine among the Gentiles.

XII

The Probative Force of Prophecies

AFTER IT HAS BEEN SHOWN that Christ predicted future events, it remains for the student to appraise their apologetical value. He must attempt to determine what type of intelligence is required to prophecy, for only in this way will their probative force be discovered.

It was shown in the last chapter that for a prediction to be a true prophecy, it must not be so cryptic that it can fit many events. It must be detailed enough so that it points to a definite event—an event which cannot be seen by natural prevision by the person making the prediction. Christ's prophecies had all the notes of true prophecies.

Rationalists reject the idea of prophecy. They hold that prophecies are made by persons who because of their unusual ability to analyze the signs of the times or, perhaps, incisively notice how history moves in cycles are able to "predict" a series of events. Sometimes they charge that ambiguous statements which could be fulfilled by the occurrence of many events are labelled as prophecies. To the rationalist, the prophet is not a person foretelling an event known only to God but a person endowed with keener and deeper prevision.

Prophecy is defined as a detailed and certain prediction of a definite future event, the foretelling of which is impossible

by natural prevision or guess because the event predicted de-
pends on many free causes for its fulfillment, and so it is pos-
sible for God alone. This definition must not be interpreted to
mean that God cannot use angels or men in making known
the substance of the prediction.

The foretelling of the future that a created agent, such as
an angel, devil or man, might make by virtue of its limited
knowledge does not answer the definition of prophecies as has
been set down. The natural knowledge of created intellects is
inextricably bound up with the cause and effect sequence and
this is not enough for prophecy. One either sees a cause in
operation in the future or he does not. If he knows what effects
have always flowed from this cause in the past, then he can
say with certitude what effects will flow from it in the future
should it operate. But in this case it would not be prophecy at
all; it would be prevision. The judgment is based on past experience. If he is not certain that a given cause will operate
at a given time in the future then he cannot foretell the resultant effect with the preciseness and certainty which is the
hallmark of a true prophecy.

Created intellects cannot prophesy because they cannot see
future events independently of their causes. They cannot see a
free cause operating because there is nothing which demands
that it should operate. It is set in motion by man's will which
is free and undetermined and, therefore, very changeable. Although angels know the future much more distinctly than
men do, they still see future events only as they are effects of
causes.

It is possible to know future events independently of causes
or as they are in themselves. "But to know the future in this
way belongs to God alone. He knows not only those events
which happen of necessity or in the majority of cases, but even
casual and chance events, for God sees all things in His eternity, which, being simple, is present to all time and embraces
all time. And, therefore, God's one glance is cast over all things

which happen in all time as present before Him; and He beholds all things as they are in themselves . . . but the mind of an angel, and every created intellect, falls far short of God's eternity; hence the future as it is in itself cannot be known by any created intellect."[1]

Several things must be said concerning the prophecies of Christ in the light of the principles which we have just discussed. The Gospels show that all of them involved free agents; they were beyond prevision and there was nothing in the past which warranted saying that these events would come to pass in these particular circumstances. Therefore, the intelligence or knowledge which was required to make them must have been more than a created or limited intelligence. The only other type of intelligence in existence is the Uncreated or Infinite Intelligence of God and so Christ's prophecies must be traced back to a divine source. They are miracles of the intellectual order. They are God's stamp of approval that the one who makes them speaks with divine authority. Since God could not authorize a lie, prophecies are proof in support of Christ's statement that He is God.

1. St. Thomas Aquinas, *Summa Theologica,* I, Ques. 57, Art. 3.

XIII

The Purpose of Christ
in Coming to Earth

It is of the utmost interest and importance to learn why
Christ came to earth. Being God, He possessed wisdom and
knowledge in an infinite degree. With Him there could be
no such thing as aimless intention or wasted effort. He had a
definite goal for everything He did.[1] In this chapter we ask
and answer what the purpose of His mission to earth was. His
miracles and prophecies furnish the credentials that this mission was fully authorized. We search the Gospels for the information we seek.

   1. The main reason why Christ came to earth was to redeem the members of the human race from their sins. Our
first parents had incurred the wrath of God on mankind by
their disobedience in the Garden of Eden. God could have
left the human race in this fallen state but Jesus Christ out of
love for men undertook to win back for them the favor of God
and to provide all with an opportunity to be saved. This theme
is repeated many times in the Gospels as these passages show:

   1. The anonymous author of that charming Second Century work entitled *Epistle to Diognetus* (ch. 8–9) was of the opinion that Christ came
as late as He did so that men might feel more deeply their corruption
and powerlessness.

"The Son of Man came to save what was lost. . . . It is not the will of your Father in heaven that a single one of these little ones should perish." [Matt. 18:11]

For God so loved the world that he gave his only-begotten Son that those who believe in him may not perish, but may have life everlasting. [John 3:16]

"The Son of Man has not come to be served, but to serve, and to give his life as a ransom for many." [Mark 10:45]

"I am the good Shepherd. The good shepherd lays down his life for his sheep." [John 10:11]

Other passages could be quoted re-emphasizing this fact. All of Christ's teaching and actions must be interpreted in light of it.

Christ reminded the members of the human race that they could never achieve true success without Him. So closely, in fact, were they to associate themselves with Him that they could be likened to branches attached to the vine. Just as the branches derive vitality and nourishment from the vine, so must people derive spiritual vitality and nourishment from Christ. But in spite of His admonition, Christ explicitly said that some would spurn this association by their disbelief and misdeeds. He said that many would take the broad road that leads to destruction; they are like the weeds that the householder permitted to grow in his field until harvest but which he finally ordered gathered up and burned. It is very clear, then, that although Christ died for all men, they are not all thereby automatically saved.

Christ not only gained merit for men by His redemptive act, but He also provided means whereby it could be channelled to them. Indeed, it is more than fitting that He who won the merit should prescribe how it is to be distributed. The accounts of the institution of several of these channels of grace are recorded in the Gospels. All of them are not listed, for St. John reminds us that many things which Jesus said and did were not committed to writing. But the presence of a few makes it eminently clear that the merit which Christ won could be gained only when men made use of the very definite means which He had instituted. In view of the indispensable character of this grace, the use or non-use of these means spells the difference between sanctification and the lack of it. Several passages prove that Christ instituted definite means of grace. He said:

"Amen, amen, I say to thee, unless a man be born again of water and the Spirit, he cannot enter into the kingdom of God." [John 3:5]

Again:

"Amen, amen I say to you, unless you eat the flesh of the Son of Man, and drink his blood, you shall not have life in you. He who eats my flesh and drinks my blood has life everlasting and I will raise him up on the last day." [John 6:55]

Then to the apostles:

"Receive the Holy Spirit; whose sins you shall forgive, they are forgiven them; and whose sins you shall retain, they are retained." [John 20:23]

These are the means available to all who meet the conditions laid down for their worthy reception.

The evidence that has been brought forth so far in this chapter makes it clear that one reason why Jesus Christ came to earth was to redeem mankind, to win merit for the members of the human race and to institute means whereby this merit could be transmitted to them.

2. We shall now see that there was also another reason for

Christ's advent to earth. This second reason is closely related to the first and is in complete harmony with it. It is this: Christ came to teach the doctrines that all men must believe and the precepts that all men must observe to be saved. He came to show them how to practice supernatural religion and thereby avail themselves of the fruits of the redemption.

About two-thirds of the Gospels are devoted to Christ's public ministry, describing His activities during the three years before His death. It is of paramount importance to notice that the Gospels picture Him as a teacher. Teaching was the core of His public ministry before His passion, overshadowing His other activities. He never neglected an opportunity to teach. Moreover, He selected seventy disciples and twelve Apostles to teach what He had imparted to them. In addition, He worked miracles to lend intensive authority to His doctrines. There are forty-two passages in the Gospels which explicitly state that Christ functioned as a teacher and there are fifty-three instances where the people refer to Christ as "Master." In the original Greek of the Gospels, the word "didascalos," i.e. "master," means "an instructor or teacher."

Once it has been established that Christ was a teacher, it is a matter of great importance to determine the nature of His teaching. His infinite wisdom will vouch for their appropriateness.

If by attentive reading, the student gathers up all of Christ's doctrines contained in the Gospels, he will notice that they readily fall into one of two categories. One category embraces the truths that man must firmly believe to be saved, and the other embraces the precepts that man must observe to be saved. In one group are the truths which are to be the object of man's intellect; in the other group are the principles of action which are to be the object of man's will. But it must not be thought that the Gospels contain exhaustively and in detail the doctrines which fill these two categories, for St. John wrote,

There are, however, many other things that Jesus did; but if every one of these should be written, not even the world itself, I think, could hold the books that would have to be written. [John 21:25]

There are a number of passages which show that Christ came to teach certain doctrines which men must believe to be saved. These are some:

He who believes in the Son has everlasting life; he who is unbelieving towards the Son shall not see life, but the wrath of God rests upon him. [John 3:36]

For God so loved the world that He gave His only-begotten Son, that those who believe in Him may not perish, but may have life everlasting. [John 3:16]

They said therefore to him, "What are we to do in order that we may perform the works of God?" In answer Jesus said to them, "This is the work of God, that you believe in him whom he has sent." [John 6:29]

Jesus answered, "Thou sayest it; I am a king. This is why I was born, and why I came into the world, to bear witness to the truth. Everyone who is of the truth hears my voice." [John 18:37]

Other similar passages could be quoted here, but these indicate sufficiently the existence of a category of doctrines of faith.

In the other group are contained the moral precepts which men must observe. Numerous passages show that Christ's teaching also embraced moral precepts. These are a few representative passages:

He answered and said, "Thou shalt love the Lord thy God with thy whole heart, and with thy whole soul, and with thy whole

strength, and with thy whole mind; and thy neighbor as thyself."
[Luke 10:27]

But Jesus said to him . . . "Thou knowest the commandments:
Thou shalt not kill, Thou shalt not commit adultery, Thou shalt
not steal, Thou shalt not bear false witness, Honor thy father and
thy mother." [Luke 18:20]

"If you love me, keep my commandments." [John 14:15]

"He who has my commandments and keeps them, he it is who
loves me. But he who loves me will be loved by my Father, and I
will love him and manifest myself to him." [John 14:21]

The Beatitudes found in the thirteenth chapter of St. Matthew's Gospel, and the Woes against the Pharisees found in
the twenty-third chapter of the same Gospel deal with the
same theme.

Notice how Christ Himself points out that His doctrines
fall into the two categories of faith and morals when He says,

"The men of Nineve will rise up in the judgment with this generation and will condemn it; for they repented at the preaching
of Jonas, and behold, a greater than Jonas is here. The queen of
the South will rise up in the judgment with this generation and
will condemn it; for she came from the ends of the earth to hear
the wisdom of Solomon, and behold, a greater than Solomon is
here. [Matt. 12:42]

The conclusion of these several observations is that one of
the reasons why Christ appeared on earth was to teach men
what they must do and believe to be saved. He came to teach
how they were to practice religion.

Christ did not intend that different sets of doctrines should
be taught in different ages or to different races. He did not

instruct those whom He commissioned to teach to revise or change His doctrines of faith and morals periodically. He taught that His teachings should be perfectly uniform in all ages and among all races. All were to accept them, for He said,

"Go, therefore, and make disciples of all nations, baptizing them in the name of the Father, and of the Son, and of the Holy Spirit, teaching them to observe all that I have commanded you." [Matt. 28:20]

After Christ had revealed to men what they must do and believe to be saved, He departed from the earth in human form. He was no longer seen teaching the multitudes. But even though the people who lived after Christ were not to see Him and to be personally instructed by Him, they, nevertheless, were obliged to live according to His doctrines. How were men to learn Christ's doctrines if He would no longer be on earth to instruct them? We shall see in the next chapter how Christ obviated this apparent difficulty and provided for the teaching of His doctrines and the administration of the channels of grace which He had instituted.

Before examining the purpose and the marks of Christ's Church, it is fitting that we should conclude this chapter with a few remarks about the non-Christian religions of the world. The principal non-Christian religions are Buddhism, Confucianism, and Mohammedanism but there are scores of smaller ones. Certain writers on comparative religions have gone to great lengths in showing what these religions have in common with Christianity. They point out that all of them have a set of beliefs and a code of morals. They show how all of them have a ritual of initiation and worship. They wish us to notice what an important part prayer plays in all of the world's religions. The same writers then go on to imply that all these similarities justify the conclusion that all religions must be put on a par with each other.

The key to the correct appraisal of the different religions is not in showing how they are alike but in how they are not alike. Christianity is different from the other religions in that it is built around a Person Who proved that He is God. The fact that Jesus Christ is divine vouches for the truthfulness of His doctrines of faith and the correctness of His precepts of morals, the efficacy of His means of sanctification and the authority of His Church. Since Buddha, Confucius and Mohammed were never able to prove that they possessed a divine mandate to found a religion, it follows that the religions which they did establish are stripped of all authority. Any truth that they do possess is either a borrowed truth or one which can be attained by the use of reason. Not only are many of their moral precepts shot through with error but some of them are scarcely more than trite proverbs. It is the likes of these that some students of comparative religions blasphemously place on an equal footing with Christianity.

Among the non-Christian religions which must be rejected as false is Judaism. At one time Judaism was a true religion, but then it was a religion of anticipation. It was essentially a preparation for the coming of the Messias. When the Messias (Jesus Christ) did come, there was no longer a need for a religion of anticipation. It was Christ's coming that made Judaism a false religion for the people of the future ages to follow.

Part Three

THE CHURCH FOUNDED BY CHRIST

XIV

The Nature of Christ's Church

AFTER CHRIST completed His work of redemption and instruction, He departed from the earth in human form. He no longer frequented the cities and villages of Palestine teaching what men must do and believe to be saved. His work was done. But Christ did not intend that only His contemporaries should benefit from His labors. These benefits were to extend to peoples living in lands far removed from His and living many centuries after Him. Distance of time and place in no way lessened the obligations which He imposed. But this presented a difficulty. How could people living after Christ receive His doctrines and merits if He was no longer on earth to transmit them?

To carry on His work of instruction and sanctification until the end of time, Christ founded a society or agency called the Church. This Church was commissioned to teach to all nations the doctrines which Christ explicitly or implicitly taught. It was not at liberty to add or to subtract from these truths. It was to hand them down integrally. To it also were confided the means through which the fruits of the redemption were to be channelled to men. In brief, the Church was to be the link between God and man.

The term "church" or the Greek word "ekklesia" is a common noun meaning "a religious gathering" or a "congregation of people." But in the New Testament and in ancient

Christian literature it means the group of those who are the followers of Christ. At times, this term is used to designate Christ's followers in a certain city or province as, for example, "The Church in Smyrna" or "The Churches of Asia." It is only in this sense that it is used in the plural. But when this term is not restricted to a place, it means the society of Christ's followers spread throughout the world. In this sense, it is never used in the plural. In this chapter, we shall show that Christ's Church is a single and definite organization. It is important to notice the clear-cut meaning of the term "church" especially since some modern writers have attempted to attach to it a meaning so vague as to embrace all who are not non-Christians.

The well-defined character of the Church is derived from the three elements of which it is constituted. These elements are incorporated in the definition which is as follows: *The Church is the society of Christ's followers who profess belief in all of His doctrines, admit the efficacy of all of His means of sanctification and are governed by superiors all of whom are subject to a supreme spiritual ruler.* These elements will be discussed in greater detail in the following chapters but we shall now sketch them to prove their existence:

1. *Believe same doctrines*—One of the elements which makes Christ's Church a unit distinct from any other religious group is that all its members believe the same set of doctrines. Christ launched the teaching effort of the Church with the instruction to the Apostles,

"Go into the whole world and preach the Gospel to every creature. He who believes and is baptized shall be saved, but he who does not believe shall be condemned." [Mark 16:15]

Several things are implied in this and similar passages. Christ clearly intimates that in His Church there would be those who must be regarded as official teachers and those who would receive this teaching. When Christ said that those who refused to accept His teaching would be condemned, He evidently eliminated them from His Church. No matter how vehemently they protest to be His followers, they contradict themselves when they claim the right to pass judgment on the acceptability of His doctrines.

2. *Means of Sanctification*—Another element that is embraced by the proper term "Christ's Church" is that the members of this society admit the efficacy and use of all the means of sanctification instituted by Christ. In establishing these means, Christ endowed them with an indispensable character. He said that without rebirth of water and the Holy Spirit, it is impossible to enter heaven; that adults would not have spiritual life unless they ate the flesh of the Son of Man and drank His blood and that sins retained on earth would be retained in heaven.

Just as Christ distinguished between the teachers and the learners of His doctrine, so He distinguished between the dispensers and the receivers of the means of grace. It is characteristic of Christ's Church that it makes available to its members all the means of sanctification confided to it. And in view of the importance of these means, the person who rejects them because he denies their efficacy, rejects membership in the organization to which they were confided.

3. *Subject to Authority*—The last element which constitutes Christ's Church as an organized society is that its members are subject to legitimate authority. Without authority no organization can maintain its individuality and identity. Christ knew this and so endowed certain members of His Church with power to rule. Over the entire Church He placed a person with supreme jurisdiction. This ruler was to be to the Church what a foundation rock is to a building, what the keeper of the keys is to a city and what a shepherd is to a flock. The implication of jurisdiction in all these figures is obvious. In Matthew 18:17 we read,

"And if he refuse to hear them, appeal to the Church, but if he refuses to hear even the Church, let him be to thee as the heathen and the publican. Amen, I say to you, whatever you bind on earth shall be bound also in heaven; and whatever you loose on earth shall be loosed also in heaven."

In this passage Christ explicitly states that recognition and subjection to the authority of the church is one of the conditions for membership in His Church.

We have seen that in the mind of Christ the term "Church" embraces three elements which make for a definite society. It does not have the vague, elusive meaning that some attach to it.

Although the Church can be proved to be a well-defined organization, the Gospels yield additional evidence concerning its nature and purpose. We consider these corollaries not only because they lead us to a better understanding of the church's scope but also to be able to answer certain critics who have raised doubts concerning their existence,

1. *The Church is Spiritual*—By spiritual we mean that the prime aim of the church is to promote the spiritual welfare of its members. It was founded for the sanctification and salvation of mankind. That Christ founded an organization whose chief interest would be things of the spirit is clear from many passages in the Gospels,—"My kingdom is not of this world" (Jn. 18:36); "The kingdom of God is at hand: repent and believe the Gospel" (Mk. 1:15). The parables of Christ repeat the spiritual character of the Church. The Church is interested in temporal affairs only insofar as they touch upon matters of faith and morals and are related to the spiritual welfare of its members.

2. *The Church is Visible*—It was pointed out above that Christ endowed certain members of the Church with jurisdiction. They were given the power to bind and to loose; they were instructed to "Feed my lambs." These words would be

absolutely meaningless if those possessing jurisdiction did not know who their subjects were. The Church therefore, must be a visible society. Christ underscored this when He said that those examining the Church would notice it to be made up of the "wheat and weeds."

The reason we call attention to the visible character of the Church is that some have denied it. Interpreting Christ's words "the kingdom of God is within you" erroneously and out of context, they have held that it is impossible to discover who the members of Christ's Church are.

3. *The Church is Perfect*—When we say that the Church is perfect we mean that she possesses all the means necessary to fulfill her mission. In this society, the members of the human race can find all that is necessary for them to reach the most perfect of all goals. These means of salvation which the Church possesses do not have to be supplemented from external sources, nor will they ever need to be revised. When we say that the Church is perfect we do not mean that all its members are perfect. Christ explicitly stated that in the kingdom of God or the Church there would be the good and the bad.

An organization is imperfect when it depends on a higher organization for its existence and operation. In this sense also, the Church is a perfect organization for it owes an account of its activity to God alone. It does not need the permission of temporal powers or civil governments to exist or to function. When the state moves to impede the church in fulfilling her mission, it does so under the presumption that it alone is a perfect organization and that all other societies, the church included, are dependent on it. To hold this opinion is error; to implement it is usurpation.

In summary we say that when Christ launched His Church some 1900 years ago, it wanted in nothing. It had definite means to achieve a definite goal and divine authorization to exist and function.

Looking into the future, Christ saw that His Church would

not be unopposed. Not only would it be impeded and persecuted by civil governments, but it would be attacked by a
different kind of foe. He saw that from time to time there
would arise false churches or spurious teaching agencies which
would function without His authorization. They would propagate doctrines in conflict with His. Some would add, some
would subtract, some would substitute under the guise of being a Church accredited by Him.

Christ saw—indeed it is obvious—what state of affairs would
develop when a score of unauthorized teaching agencies began
diffusing their own peculiar set of doctrines. Confusion and
uncertainty would result. Bewildered by the lack of uniformity that the conflict of contradictory doctrines thrust upon
him, the ordinary inquirer would soon despair of knowing
truth in religious matters. He would soon give up the search
for finding the true Church. The end result would be that the
effectiveness of much of Christ's efforts would be nullified, for
of what good to me are the facilities of a fine organization—
its authority to teach and to distribute the means of grace—if
I cannot find it. Christ clearly saw that a way had to be found
to distinguish truth from error especially since the most difficult error to identify is the error that imitates truth.

To protect the honest inquirer, that is, to lead him to the
Church which He had founded, Christ impressed on it four
marks of identification. By means of these marks the authentic
teaching agency set up by Christ could be easily distinguished
from false teaching agencies. The use of the marks makes it
possible not only for the learned to find the true Church—not
only for those who have the time and ability—but for anyone
who is serious enough to investigate. Indeed this is according
to common sense for Christ founded His Church not merely
to benefit a special class or privileged group but for all men
who would live on earth after Him.

Nowhere in the Gospels is it recorded that Christ gave His
Church a technical or proper name. And it is easy to sur-

mise why He did not. There is nothing about a proper name which prevents it from being appropriated or copied by a false church. Instead of a name He gave it four marks. *A mark is defined as a fixed characteristic given by Christ to His Church as a whole to serve as a means of easily distinguishing it from unauthorized agencies which attempt to usurp its prerogatives.* To be clearcut, foolproof means of identifying the true Church, these marks must have certain characteristics: (a) They must be such that no false church can copy them. (b) Since the Church must be able to be found by men of every century, these marks must be permanent, that is, the Church can in no way lose them or have them stripped away from her. (c) They must be intellectually visible.

Our task in the following chapters will be to discover precisely what the four marks of the true Church are. We shall examine Christ's words in this matter and then search history for the Church which possesses these marks.[1] This church will not be buried in history. Since it is a permanent society, it exists in the world today. That Church and only that Church which possesses the four marks of identification will be the one authorized by Christ to teach, to sanctify and to rule in His Name.

1. Lest someone should think that this method is arbitrary and an innovation of recent centuries, it must be remarked that all four marks are implicitly though clearly contained in the seven authentic epistles of St. Ignatius of Antioch who died in *c.* 107. The importance of the Apostolic Fathers lies in the fact that they did not speculate but transmitted teachings as they learned them.

XV

The Mark of Apostolicity

IT WAS POINTED OUT in the last chapter that Christ appeared
on earth to teach men what they must do and believe in order
to be saved. He intended that the same doctrines should be
received by all races in all ages, and to diffuse them, He founded a church—or teaching agency. It is the purpose of these
chapters, therefore, to discover the marks by which Christ's
Church is distinguished from all spurious teaching agencies.

During His public ministry Christ taught thousands of people, and the doctrines which He taught He wanted transmitted to others. But nowhere in the Gospels did Christ issue
to His listeners an indiscriminate commission to teach in His
Name. He did not invest each and every one of them with the
authority to instruct others. For this task He especially selected, trained and commissioned only a few of the great number who listened to Him, as shown by these passages:

"You have not chosen me, but I have chosen you, and have appointed you that you should go and bear fruit, and that your fruit
should remain." [John 15:16]

Now after this the Lord appointed seventy-two others, and sent
them forth two by two before him into every town and place
where he himself was about to come. And he said to them, "The
harvest indeed is abundant, but the laborers are few. Pray there-

fore the Lord of the harvest to send forth laborers into his harvest."
[Luke 10:1–11]

And going up a mountain, he called to him men of his own choos-
ing, and they came to him. And he appointed twelve that they
might be with him and that he might send them forth to preach . . .
There were Simon, to whom he gave the name Peter; and James
the son of Zebedee, and John the brother of James (these he sur-
named Boanerges, that is, Sons of Thunder); and Andrew, and
Philip, and Bartholomew, and Matthew, and Thomas, and James
the son of Alpheus, and Thaddeus, and Simon the Cananean, and
Judas Iscariot, who also betrayed him. [Mark 3:13–19]

The disciples therefore rejoiced at the sight of the Lord. He therefore said to them again, "Peace be to you. As the Father has sent
me, I also send you." [John 20:21]

In this connection the etymology of the word "apostle" is
interesting. It is derived from a Greek verb which means "to
send on a mission." If Christ had commissioned all who listened to Him to teach, the Gospels would refer to them all as
"apostles." But such is not the case. This term is reserved only
for the members of the group whom Christ selected to teach
in His Name. He pronounced severe penalties against anyone
who refused to receive His doctrines as the Apostles taught
them.

Although all the Apostles received their commission to teach
directly from Christ, the Gospels indicate that the exercise of
this teaching office was not left entirely to the discretion of
each Apostle. Christ introduced a new element into the structure of this teaching group. It pertained to the manner in
which the individual Apostles were to exercise their commission. The next two Gospel passages which will be discussed
prove the existence of this new element.

In the sixteenth chapter of St. Matthew's Gospel there is
contained this passage:

Now Jesus, having come into the district of Caesarea Philippi, began to ask his disciples, saying, "Who do men say the Son of Man
is?" But they said, "Some say, John the Baptist; and others, Elias;
and others, Jeremias, or one of the prophets." He said to them,
"But who do you say that I am?" Simon Peter answered and said,
"Thou art the Christ, the Son of the living God." Then Jesus
answered and said, "Blessed art thou, Simon Bar-Jona, for flesh
and blood has not revealed this to thee, but my Father in heaven.
And I say to thee, thou art Peter, and upon this rock I will build
my Church, and the gates of hell shall not prevail against it. And
I will give thee the keys of the kingdom of heaven; and whatever
thou shalt bind on earth shall be bound in heaven, and whatever
thou shalt loose on earth shall be loosed in heaven." [Matt.
16:13–19]

The importance of this passage is indicated by the vast
amount of comment which it has caused. Some have expended
much effort in attempting to weaken its force; others have
labored to uphold it. Some have attempted to dispatch quickly all comment on it by saying that it was not in the original
Gospel of St. Matthew. They hold that it was a subsequent
addition to the text. But those who advance this thesis are
handicapped at every turn in their attempt to prove it. The
modern critical editions of the Greek New Testament show
that the manuscript evidence is against it. The editions of
Tischendorf (8th), Gregory, Westcott-Hort, Von Soden, Nestle
and Merk prove that there is no doubt concerning the authenticity of this passage.

An exegesis of the passage under consideration does not
support the interpretation of those investigators who say that
Christ was addressing not only Peter but all the Apostles
through Peter when He promised to confer privileges. They
say that Peter was merely a spokesman for the Apostles. But
the Evangelist shows that the Apostles did not need a spokesman. When Christ asked them who the people said the Son

of Man was, they all answered for themselves. When Christ asked them for their opinion, only Peter answered, saying that He was the Son of God. In the reply to this confession, Christ singled out Peter from among the rest, for He prefaced His remarks by saying:

"Blessed are thou, Simon Bar-Jona."

Then in the verses which follow, Christ addressed Peter alone, for seven times He used only the second person singular pronoun. In English, the pronoun "you" can be either singular or plural, but in the Greek language a different word is used for each. In this passage, only the second person singular is used, thus showing that Christ was speaking solely to Peter.

Some investigators say that when Christ said,

"Thou art Peter, and upon this rock I will build my Church,"

He meant that the foundation of His Church would be the rocklike firmness of Peter's faith or confession. Others say that at the moment Christ said "this rock," He was either pointing to Himself or to a nearby rock. But there is no evidence to support any of these interpretations. They are purely arbitrary. On this point, Plummer, an Anglican exegete, says,

All attempts to explain the "Rock" in any other way than as referring to Peter have ignominiously failed. Neither the confession of Peter nor the faith of Peter is an adequate explanation.[1]

And O. Pfleiderer of the non-Catholic Tübingen School writes,

In spite of all Protestant attempts to weaken its force, it cannot be doubted that this passage (Mt. 16:16 ff) contains the solemn proclamation of the primacy of Peter. He is declared to be the foundation of the Church, the bearer of the keys and the sovereign

1. Lebreton, *History of the Primitive Church* (New York; Macmillan, 1941), I, 126.

lawgiver, whose precepts and prohibitions have the force of divinely sanctioned laws.[2]

Christ stated positively what He meant when He said, "this rock" for He changed Simon's name to Peter which means rock. Fitting this change of name into the passage in question it would read, "Thou art a rock (Peter) and it is upon this rock that I will build my Church."

The foundation of the Church was to be the person of Peter, not the faith of Peter for an inflexible and impersonal profession of faith could not exercise the judgment which is necessary to decide when to use the authority of binding and of loosing. Christ's use of the pronoun "thou" confirms this interpretation.

In the passage being discussed, Christ pointed out Peter's capacity in the Church. He was to be to the Church what a foundation stone is to a building. As the foundation lends stability and unity to a building, so Peter was to lend stability to the Church. The foundation of organized society is authority. Without authority an organization has neither stability nor unity. When Christ said that Peter was to be the foundation stone of the Church, He implied that Peter was to possess the fundamental authority in the Church.

By the will of Christ, Peter was to be to the Church what the keeper of the keys is to a house or city. In ancient times keys were used as a symbol of jurisdiction. The one who held the keys possessed the authority to admit or to exclude from a house or city whomever he wished. When Christ promised to give to Peter the keys to the kingdom of heaven, He thereby designated Peter as the one who would have the fundamental jurisdiction in His Church. Christ likewise implied that Peter's jurisdiction was to extend over the whole Church for He in no way restricted it. He told Peter that whatever law he would see fit to decree, to bind or loose the consciences of

2. Brunsmann-Preuss, *Fundamental Theology* (St. Louis; Herder, 1931), III, 119.

men, would have the same binding force as though it were decreed by God in heaven.

The passage in St. Matthew's Gospel, which has just been discussed, fully warrants the conclusion that Christ promised to Peter alone, from among the Apostles, a primacy, not merely of honor, but of jurisdiction over the whole Church which He was to establish.

The account of the fulfillment of the promise of the primacy is contained in this passage of St. John's Gospel:

When therefore they had breakfasted, Jesus said to Simon Peter, "Simon, son of John, dost thou love me more than these do?" He said to him, "Yes, Lord, thou knowest that I love thee." He said to him, "Feed my lambs." He said to him a second time, "Simon, son of John, dost thou love me?" He said to him, "Yes, Lord, thou knowest that I love thee." He said to him, "Feed my lambs." A third time he said to him, "Simon, son of John, dost thou love me?" Peter was grieved because he said to him a third time, "Dost thou love me?" And he said to him, "Lord, thou knowest all things, thou knowest that I love thee." And He said to him, "Feed my sheep." [John 21:15-18]

In the passage which has just been quoted, it is impossible not to understand to whom Christ is speaking. He addressed Himself to Peter alone and not to the Apostles as a group. He called Peter by name three times and set him apart from the others by asking him,

"Dost thou care for me more than these others?" And when Peter affirmed his love for Christ with growing intensity, Christ used the imperative singular in saying, "Feed my lambs," and, "Feed my sheep."

What did Christ mean when He wished Peter to feed His flock? In its expanded form, the command which Christ addressed to Peter meant that Peter was to be to the members of the Church what a shepherd is to a sheepfold. Just as a shepherd has a duty to feed and protect the members of the flock, so does he have the right to be obeyed by them in matters which pertain to their welfare. The shepherd has the right to take the means that will promote the well-being of his charges. Now Christ intended that Peter's rights and duties should parallel the rights of a shepherd over the flock. By this figure, Christ obviously conferred on Peter jurisdiction over the entire Church.

A third proof of the superior position of Peter among the Apostles can be gathered from a careful examination of the four catalogues of the Apostles found in the New Testament. The force of this argument is best brought out when the lists are set down in parallel columns. It will be noticed that the Evangelists do not write down these names in a haphazard fashion. They were careful in making their listing. Each catalogue is broken down into three groups of four Apostles and each sub-division is always headed by the same man. In the light of this care, it is not mere coincidence that in each list Peter's name is always first and Judas's name is always last.

Mt. 10:2	Mk. 3:2	Lk. 6:14	Acts 1:13
Peter	Peter	Peter	Peter
Andrew	James Greater	Andrew	John
James Greater	John	James Greater	James Greater
John	Andrew	John	Andrew
Philip	Philip	Philip	Philip
Bartholomew	Bartholomew	Bartholomew	Thomas
Thomas	Matthew	Matthew	Bartholomew
Matthew	Thomas	Thomas	Matthew
James Less	James Less	James Less	James Less
Thaddeus	Thaddeus	Simon	Simon
Simon	Simon	Thaddeus	Thaddeus
Judas	Judas	Judas	Now a suicide

In Matt. 10:2 we read,

Now these are the names of the twelve apostles: first Simon, who is called Peter, and his brother Andrew; James the son of Zebedee, and his brother John. . . .

When the Evangelist calls Peter the "first," he is not using the numeral adjective for, if he were, he would have continued the enumeration with the words, "second, third, fourth, etc." But he does not do so. It cannot refer to the order in which the Apostles were called for the word "first" is used only for Peter and he was not the first one called. Andrew was called before Peter as the Fourth Gospel (Jn. 1:40) clearly indicates. He was not the one regarded to be foremost in the affections of Christ for John repeatedly calls himself the "disciple whom Jesus loved." The only remaining explanation is that the word "first" refers to Peter's rank among the Apostles and is but another indication of the primacy of jurisdiction which Christ had given to him.

Another indication of Peter's position of singular importance among the Apostles can be gathered from the number of times that the Evangelists take notice of his activities. If Peter were not superior to them, there would have been no reason to give him as much attention as was given to him. Notice how often Peter's name recurs in the Gospels and Acts of the Apostles in comparison with the names of the other Apostles.

	Matt.	Mark	Luke	John	Acts	Totals
Peter	26	24	29	41	59	179
John	3	10	7		10	30
James Greater	3	11	5		5	24
Judas	4	3	4	9	3	23
Philip	1	1	1	12	1	16
Andrew	2	4	1	5	1	13
Thomas	1	1	1	8	1	12
James Less	3	3	1		2	9
Matthew	3	2	3		1	9
Bartholomew	1	1	1		1	4
Thaddeus	1	1	1		1	4
Simon	1	1	1		1	4

Simple arithmetic reveals that Peter's name recurs 179 times while the names of all the other Apostles combined recur 149 times. It is not without reason that Peter's name should appear almost six times more than any other Apostle.

With the conclusion of the examination of the meaning of the passages from the Gospels, it can be seen that although thousands listened to Christ, He commissioned only a few of them to teach in His Name. But the few who were commissioned to teach were to exercise their commission under the primacy of jurisdiction which Christ promised and conferred only on Peter.

The passages which prove that Christ conferred on Peter a primacy of jurisdiction, contain one of the four marks by which the True Church can be distinguished from all false churches. This mark of identification consists in the fact that since Christ established His Church on Peter, the True Church is that Church which can prove that Peter was its first ruler. If a given church does not go back to Peter, it must be labelled as an unauthorized teaching agency. This mark is known as the mark of apostolicity, and the only way to discover which Church possesses it is by historical inquiry.

The Identification of the Church with the Mark of Apostolicity

It is not an intricate process to discover which church of today goes back to the person of Peter. It is a purely historical study which involves the tracing of the different churches from their point of origin to the present time.

Since Peter was given a primacy over the entire Church, it is important to trace his activity as the head of the Church. And, more precisely, it must be determined where he set up his See. If Christ intended that people should look to Peter for guidance in such an important matter as salvation, they must know where to find him. But if this place is indefinite, then the effectiveness of having a supreme guide is lost. Hence, the importance of discovering where Peter set up his See and where he died.

There were several ancient witnesses who were qualified, by study or personal experience, to speak on the whereabouts of Peter after he was invested with power. The first of these was St. Ignatius of Antioch, who was martyred, probably in the Colosseum, in about 107 A.D.[3] On his way from Syria to Rome he dispatched seven letters[4] to various Christian communities and individuals. In his letter to the Romans, he writes,

Make petition, then, to the Lord for me, so that by these means I may be made a sacrifice to God. I do not command you, as Peter and Paul did. They were Apostles; I am a condemned man.[5]

The implication of this sentence is that Peter exercised authority in Rome. The casualness with which St. Ignatius speaks of Peter shows that he is not telling the Romans something which they did not already know.

Another witness to the whereabouts of Peter was St. Irenaeus, whose travel, study and acquaintance with primitive tradition makes his testimony invaluable [6] He writes:

Matthew also issued a written Gospel among the Hebrews in their own dialect, while Peter and Paul were preaching in Rome and establishing the foundations of the Church there.[7]

The testimony of the third witness has a double probative force. The use of the proper name "Babylon," which occurs

3. Cayre, *Manual of Patrology,* trans. by (Tournai; Howitt, 1936), I, 64.

4. These letters were authenticated by Lightfoot in his work, *Apostolic Fathers* (London; MacMillan, 1885), Vol. I, Pt. 2, pp. 315–414.

5. *Ad Romanos,* ch. 4, trans. by Walsh in "Fathers of the Church" series (New York; Cima, 1947).

6. Cf. Tertullian *Adv. Valentineanos* ch. 5.

7. *Adversus Haereses* Bk. III. 1. 1.

in the First Epistle of Peter has caused much discussion. A monograph would be required to exhaust the arguments which have been produced to fix its meaning. Suffice it here to produce the testimony of Clement of Alexandria (c. 150–c. 211) on this point. It is said that,

He also says that Peter mentions Mark in his first epistle and that he composed it in Rome itself, referring to the city metaphorically as Babylon, in the words, "The elect one, Babylon, greets you and Marcus my son."[8]

The double force of this quotation lies in the fact that it contains the testimony of both Peter and Clement.

The last of the ancient witnesses to be cited concerning Peter's whereabouts is Eusebius, the historian of Caesarea in Palestine. He was in a favorable position to test the truth of many statements current in his day not only by his extensive travel but also by his access to the famous library at Caesarea. He summarizes the tradition in regard to Peter when he says:

Close after him in the same reign of Claudius, the Providence of the universe in its goodness and love toward men, guided to Rome, as against a gigantic pest on life, the great and mighty Peter, who for his virtues was the leader of all the other Apostles.[9]

And speaking of the tradition concerning Mark, he says:

Tradition says that he came to Rome in the reign of Claudius to speak to Peter, who was at that time preaching to those there.[10]

Peter's presence in Rome is also an archeological question upon which findings in the catacombs of Rome have shed some

8. *H.E.* Bk. II. 15. 2.
9. *H.E.* Bk. II. 14. 16.
10. *H.E.* Bk. II. 18. 1.

light.[11] On this theme the eminent archeologist, Orazio Marucchi writes:

. . . these dates are not absolutely incontestable, but the principal fact of Peter's coming to Rome is historical and capable of the most rigorous and scientific proof.[12]

The testimony which has been reproduced above clearly shows that after Peter had received a primacy of jurisdiction from Christ, he eventually went to Rome.[13] The testimony quoted here to prove it is important for several reasons. It is the testimony of witnesses who lived in widely separated parts of the Roman Empire, none of whom were natives of Rome.[14] It covers the entire ante-Nicene period of Christianity with nothing in ancient literature to contradict it.

The Place of Peter's Death

In order to determine the permanent See of Peter, it is important to discover over what See he ruled when he died. It is certain that he exercised a primacy of jurisdiction at Jerusalem. Tradition reports that he spent some time at Antioch in Syria. It is definite that he eventually set up his See in Rome. One way to show that he did not transfer his See from Rome is to prove that he died in Rome. The testimony of antiquity is agreed that he also died in Rome. The North African writer, Tertullian, says:

11. Marucchi, *Manual of Christian Archeology,* trans. by Vecchierello (Paterson; St. Anthony Guild Press, 1935), p. 24.

12. *Ibid.,* p. 22.

13. For a detailed study of Peter's presence in Rome, read T. B. Livius' *St. Peter, Bishop of Rome* (London; Burns, Oates, 1888).

14. In ancient times, cities claimed famous men as natives. Since none of the above witnesses were natives of Rome, they cannot be accused of falsely claiming Peter as one of their own townsmen.

Since moreover, you are close upon Italy, you have Rome, from which there comes even into our own hands the very authority (of the apostles themselves). How happy its church, on which apostles poured forth all their doctrine along with their blood; where Peter endures a passion like his Lord's.[15]

Let us see . . . what utterance the Romans give, so very near, to whom Peter and Paul conjointly bequeathed the gospel even sealed with their own blood.[16]

Perhaps the best known reference to the death of Peter at Rome in ancient literature is the one found in the Ecclesiastical History of Eusebius. The opening remarks of this passage tell of the persecution of Nero (64–69 A.D.). The reference reads as follows:

It is related that in his [Nero's] time, Paul was beheaded in Rome itself and that Peter likewise was crucified and the title "Peter and Paul" which is still given in the cemeteries there, confirms the story, no less than does the writer of the Church named Caius, who lived when Zepherinus was bishop of Rome (199–217). Caius in a discussion with Proclus, speaks as follows of the places where the sacred relics of the Apostles in question are deposited: "But I can point out the trophies [meaning tombs] of the Apostles, for if you go to the Vatican or to the Ostian Way, you will find the trophies of those who founded this Church." And that they both were martyred at the same time, Dionysius, bishop of Corinth, affirms in this passage of his correspondence with the Romans. "By so great an admonition, you bound together the foundation of the Romans and the Corinthians by Peter and Paul, for both of them taught together in our Corinth and were our founders, and together also taught in Italy in the same place and were martyred at the same time."[17]

15. *De Praescriptione Haerticorum* Ch. 36.
16. *Adversus Marcionem* Bk. IV. 5.
17. *H.E.* Bk. II. 25. 5–8.

This reference not only contains the central fact that Peter died in Rome, but it also gives the approximate date and the manner of his death. It is certain that St. Peter's relics were first buried in a surface cemetery on the Cornelian Way which was the north boundary of Nero's gardens.[18] It was situated in that section of Rome known even in ancient times as the Vatican. Inscriptions found in 1921 show that, for some reason unknown to us, they were transferred temporarily to the cemetery of St. Sebastian *ad catacumbas* on the Appian Way.[19] They were later returned to their original resting place on the Vatican. Several basilicas were built over this tomb. Archeologists today have not been able to determine at what depth the Apostle's relics were reburied when the present basilica was built. This edifice was completed in 1612. With the proof that Peter died in Rome, the definiteness concerning his whereabouts after he received the primacy becomes more entrenched than ever.

Peter's Successors

The next task in the inquiry is to ascertain who were Peter's successors in the See of Rome, for the Church which goes back in unbroken succession to the person of Peter is the Church which has the identifying mark of apostolicity. Space does not permit the inclusion of quotations which give the names of only one or two successors, for scores of such quotations are available. But, fortunately, several ancient writers have made catalogues of the successors of Peter from the time of Peter down to their own day. The first of these writers is St. Irenaeus of Lyons. He counts up the rulers of the See of Rome from the time of Peter down to about the year 180 A.D. This is St. Irenaeus' list:

18. *I Monumenti Cristiani*, Grossi-Condi S.J. (Rome, 1923), p. 301.
19. *Nuovo Bullettino d'Archeologia Cristiana*, Nos. 1916 to 1921.

The blessed Apostles, having founded and built up the church, committed into the hands of Linus the office of the episcopate ... to him succeeded Anacletus, and after him in the third place, Clement was allotted the bishopric ... to this Clement there succeeded Evaristus. Alexander followed Evaristus. Then sixth from the Apostles Sixtus was appointed; after him Telesphorus who was gloriously martyred; then Hyginus, after him Pius, then after him Anicetus, Soter having succeeded Anicetus, Eleutherius does now in the twelfth place from the Apostles, hold the inheritance of the episcopate. In this order and by this succession the ecclesiastical tradition from the Apostles and the preaching of the truth has come down to us.[20]

A second list is found in the writing of St. Optatus of Milevis. He reproduces the list of St. Irenaeus and extends it to about the year 366 A.D. This is St. Optatus' list:

You cannot deny that you know that the episcopal Chair was first assigned to Peter, in the city of Rome, in which sat Peter, the head of all the Apostles. Peter, therefore, first filled that pre-eminent Chair, which is the first of the marks of the Church; Linus succeeded Peter, Clement succeeded Linus, (then these succeeded each other in the following order): Anacletus, Evaristus, Alexander, Sixtus, Telesphorus, Hyginus, Anicetus, Pius, Soter, Eleutherius, Victor, Zepherinus, Callixtus, Urbanus, Pontianus, Anterus, Fabianus, Cornelius, Lucius, Stephan, Sixtus, Dionysius, Felix, Eutychianus, Caius, Marcellinus, Marcellus, Eusebius, Miltiades, Sylvester, Marcus, Julius, Liberius, Damasus. The successor of Damasus was Siricius, who is now our fellow bishop and with whom the whole world, together with us, is in agreement in one fellowship of communion by mutual exchange of formal correspondence.[21]

Another catalogue was compiled by St. Augustine, the illustrious bishop of Hippo in Numidia. He reproduces the catalogue and extends it to about the year 400 A.D. He writes:

20. *Adversus Haereses* Bk. III. 3. 3.
21. *De Schismate Donatistarum* Bk. II. 1–3.

For if the lineal order of the succession of bishops is to be taken into account, with how much certainty and true benefit do we begin count from Peter himself, to whom, as bearing the figure of the whole Church, the Lord said, "Upon this rock I will build My Church, and the gates of hell shall not prevail against it." . . . The successor of Peter was Linus, Clement [succeeded] Linus, [the other unbroken successors were] Anacletus, Evaristus, Sixtus, Telesphorus, Hyginus, Anicetus, Pius, Soter, Alexander, Victor, Zepherinus, Calixtus, Urbanus, Pontianus, Antherus, Fabianus, Cornelius, Lucius, Stephan, Sixtus, Dionysius, Felix, Eutychianus, Caius, Marcellus, Eusebius, Melchiades, Sylvester, Marcus, Julius, Liberius, Damasus, Siricius, Anastasius.[22]

The documents from which these lists were taken are authentic. They are sufficient to establish the fact that the names of Peter's ante-Nicene successors were well known in ancient times. But in the middle of the Nineteenth Century there was made a discovery in connection with this matter which is of rare historical worth. It was made in 1854 by J. B. De Rossi in the catacombs of St. Callixtus on the Appian Way just outside of Rome. He found there a subterranean crypt lost for centuries and containing the tombs of certainly five and perhaps six popes of the Third Century. The pontiffs in question were Anterus who died in 235 A.D., Pontian in 236, Fabian in 250, Lucius in 257, Eutychian in 283 and perhaps also Urban. In another part of the same cemetery were found the tombs of Cornelius who died in 252, Caius in 296 and Eusebius in 310. Notice how neatly these names fit into the lists of Optatus and Augustine. There were ten other vaults in the same "crypt of the popes," but time had stripped them of all means of identification. We cannot advance beyond conjecture in determining who were interred there but the possibility that they were other early pontiffs cannot be eliminated.

There are several other catalogues[23] of the bishops of Rome, but these will suffice to show that the lineage of St. Peter's suc-

22. *Ep.* 53 *ad Generosum.*
23. Epiphanius, *Haereses* Bk. I. 2. 6.

cessors in the See of Rome was unbroken down to the Fifth
Century.

There is no serious difficulty[24] in showing that the line of
Peter's successors is unbroken from the Fifth Century down
to the present day. The historical evidence for the continuity
of this line is much more abundant[25] and was more easily preserved after the Fifth Century than before. It was reliable
enough that even Macaulay felt perfectly justified in writing:

There is not and there never was on this earth, a work of human
policy so well deserving of examination as the Roman . . . Church.
. . . The proudest royal houses are but of yesterday when compared
with the line of the Supreme Pontiffs. That line we trace back in
unbroken series from the Pope who crowned Napoleon in the nineteenth century to the Pope who crown Pepin in the eighth; and
far beyond the time of Pepin the august dynasty extends. . . .[26]

From the evidence which has been presented in these pages,
one is warranted to conclude that there is an unbroken line of
successors from St. Peter down to the present bishop of Rome.
It is the Roman Church, therefore, which goes back to the very
person of Peter and so possesses the identifying mark of apostolicity.

The Jurisdiction of the Bishop of Rome

Usually treated in connection with the inquiry into the
apostolicity of the Church is the question of the jurisdiction
of the bishops of Rome as successors of St. Peter. A variety of

24. The residence of the bishops of Rome at Avignon in France does
not militate against the unbroken lineage of Peter's successors. Even
though they lived at Avignon, they were still bishops of Rome, just as a
king is still king when he sojourns outside his realm.

25. Read Lindsay, *Evidence for the Papacy* (London; Longmans,
Green & Co., 1870).

26. *Essay on Ranke's History of the Popes,* Thomas Babington Macaulay 1800–1859, an important English writer and not a member of the
Roman Church.

theories have been put forth on this question, but like all historical theories they must be modified by the facts. In proceeding with this inquiry, the student should pay special attention to the Will of Christ in this matter. However, much can be learned by noting whether or not the bishops of Rome did exercise a primacy of jurisdiction over the whole Church and whether or not the other bishops of the world recognized this exercise as legitimate.

First of all must be regarded the Will of Christ concerning the jurisdiction of St. Peter's successors.[27] The foundation of Christ's Church ought to exist as long as the Church itself exists. Since Christ intended that His Church should endure for all ages, it follows that its foundation must exist for all ages. Now, the foundation of Christ's Church was a man who was given a primacy of jurisdiction. As long as the Church exists, it must rest on one who has such a primacy. The man who was originally given this primacy of jurisdiction was Peter. But, since Peter is no longer alive, and since it is still necessary for the Church to have for its foundation one who possesses a primacy of jurisdiction, it follows that Peter's successors have this power. The bishops of Rome as the successors of Peter possess the same jurisdiction which Christ intended Peter to have.

There is another reason for saying that Peter's successors possess a primacy of power. On the occasion of the promising and conferring of the primacy of jurisdiction on Peter, Christ referred to the organization which Peter was to rule as "My Church," the "Kingdom of Heaven," and "My Flock." Since Christ used these terms without qualification, He could not possibly have meant that it embraced only the members of the Church who were Peter's contemporaries. By His Kingdom and His Flock He meant all the people who would ever enter the Church during the succeeding ages. Therefore, when Christ conferred upon Peter a primacy of jurisdiction, He in

27. Zapelena S.J., *De Ecclesia Christi* (Rome, 1932), p. 125.

reality established a permanent office in the Church and Peter was but its first occupant. Since this office was not to go out of existence with Peter's death, it follows that Peter's successors have the same primacy that Christ wished Peter to have. The power automatically goes with the position of being Peter's successor.

There are instances in ancient history which reflect the relationship which existed between the bishop of Rome and the bishops of the rest of the world. The earliest of these dates back to the First Century. One of the oldest writings of the Christian Era, the First Letter of Clement of Rome to the Corinthians,[28] written about 96/98 A.D. deals with this question. There was a sedition in Corinth. Certain factions would not obey their ruler. To heal this division, Clement, the bishop of Rome, sent a letter to the Corinthians in which he demanded, under penalty of sin, that they obey his request for peace. He reminded them that God spoke through him and that he had an obligation to act in circumstances such as these.

Dionysius, bishop of Corinth (c. 170), in a passage preserved by Eusebius,[29] has reflected the attitude of the Corinthians towards this letter of Clement. If Clement's letter were a usurpation, they would have rejected it. But Dionysius says that they accepted it and read it at services on Sunday. This shows that though the people of Corinth had a bishop of their own, they recognized the right of the bishop of Rome to speak with authority outside his own diocese. The fact that Clement does not have to explain his interference shows that the Corinthians were already acquainted with the superior position of the bishop of Rome when they received Clement's letter.

J. B. Lightfoot has admitted[30] that the Letter of Clement to

28. A copy of this letter was discovered by Bryennios in 1875 in the library attached to the Church of the Holy Sepulchre, which is in the Greek quarter of Constantinople.

29. *H.E.* IV. 23. 11. Cf. also *H.E.* IV. 22. 1; *Adv. Her.* III. 3. 3.

30. *Apostolic Fathers* (Macmillan, 1885), Vol. I, Pt. 1, p. 70. Lightfoot was a prominent Anglican scholar and known among non-Catholic scholars for his conservative views.

the Corinthians is an authentic case of the bishop of Rome claiming a primacy of jurisdiction.

Another witness of the position of the Church of Rome and, therefore, of the bishop of Rome, was St. Ignatius of Antioch. The seven letters which he dispatched while on his way to Rome have similar introductions, except the one to the Romans (written c. 107 A.D.). Its tone is much more elevated than the rest. In it, Ignatius sings the praises of the Roman Church in these terms.

Ignatius Theophorus . . . to the Church in the place of the country of the Romans which holds the primacy. I salute you in the name of Jesus Christ, the Son of the Father, You are a Church worthy of God, worthy of honor, felicitation and praise, worthy of attaining to God, a Church without blemish, which holds the primacy of the community of love. . . .[31]

The interesting phrase here is "the Church . . . which holds the primacy." In view of the clear claim of a primacy of jurisdiction contained in the Letter of Clement to the Corinthians and the fact that Ignatius speaks only to the Romans in this manner, the term "primacy" must be interpreted to mean a primacy of jurisdiction until the contrary can be proved.

The First Letter of Clement showed the jurisdiction of the bishop of Rome over one community outside his diocese; the testimony of Ignatius implied the superiority of the Roman bishop over several dioceses. But, in the last decade of the Second Century, there came to a head a situation which showed the authority of the bishop of Rome over Christians from Lyons in Gaul to Syria. At this time there was a controversy between the East and West over the date on which to celebrate Easter. The bishops of Asia[32] disagreed with the bishop of Rome on this liturgical point. When much discussion did not

31. *Ad Romanos,* Introduction.
32. This is the Roman province of Asia. It was one of the most important Roman provinces and situated on the Aegean Sea in the western part of what is now Asia Minor.

settle the question, Victor, the bishop of Rome (c. 189–199 A.D.), decided to settle it with authority. He threatened to excommunicate every Asiatic bishop who would not agree with him. Eusebius records this when he writes:

Upon this Victor, who presided at Rome, immediately tried to cut off from the common unity the dioceses of all Asia, together with the adjacent churches,[33] on the grounds of heterodoxy, and he indited letters announcing that all the Christians there were absolutely excommunicated.[34]

Eusebius goes on to relate how many bishops entreated Victor to reconsider his threat. They asked him to weigh well the effects that such an excommunication would have. Notice, however, that not a single one of the bishops disputed Victor's right to carry out his threat, thus clearly indicating that they recognized that Victor, in his capacity as the bishop of Rome, possessed a primacy of jurisdiction.

One of the bishops who entreated Victor not to be so drastic in settling the Easter controversy was St. Irenaeus of Lyons (c. 130–203 A.D.). He was known to have been acquainted with the tradition of the different parts of the Christian world.[35] His intercession on behalf of the Eastern bishops is evidence in favor of the primacy of the bishop of Rome. He gives evidence on this subject in his writing against the Gnostic heretics. He states:

But as it would be a very long task to enumerate in such a volume as this the successions of all the churches, we put to confusion all those who assemble in unauthorized meetings by indicating the tradition derived from the Apostles, of the very great, the very ancient and universally known church founded and constituted at Rome by the most glorious apostles Peter and Paul; as also the faith preached to men, which comes down to our times by means of the succession of the bishops. For it is a matter of necessity that

33. This means a Christian community.
34. *H.E.* V. xxiv. 9 (Loeb Ed., Vol. 1; Ug. 509).
35. Cf. Tertullian, *Adv. Valentineanos* Ch. 5.

every church should agree with this one on account of its pre-eminent authority.[36]

This last statement that: "it is a matter of necessity that every church should agree with this one on account of its pre-eminent authority" is generally accepted to mean that in the mind of St. Irenaeus the bishop of Rome possessed a primacy of jurisdiction over all the other bishops of the Church.

St. Cyprian, the bishop of Carthage (c. 210–258 A.D.) is well known for his writing on the unity of the Church. In developing his theme he gives important testimony concerning the superior position of the bishop of Rome. Cyprian produces several reasons for saying that the true Church must be a unity. His most famous argument is that the Church is one because it was founded on Peter. Peter's See possesses a primacy which makes it the source of unity for the entire Church. Cyprian is clearly a witness to the extraordinary rank of the Roman Pontiff when he writes:

Cornelius was made bishop of Rome by the judgment of God and His Christ, by the testimony of almost all the clergy, by the suffrage of all the people who were present at the time when no one had been made bishop before him; when the place of Peter and the Rank of the Apostolic Chair was vacant.[37]

Moreover, after all this, a pseudo-bishop having been set up for themselves by heretics, they dare to sail, and to carry letters from some schismatics and profane persons, to the Chair of Peter, and to the Principal Church, whence the unity of the priesthood took its rise; nor do they consider that the Romans are those whose faith was praised in the preaching of the Apostle.[38]

Since it was proved that Christ conferred on Peter a primacy of jurisdiction, it must be said that when Cyprian writes that the bishop of Rome sits in the Chair of Peter, he means that

36. *Adversus Haereses* III. 3. 3. M.P.G., Vol. 7, Col. 849.
37. *Ep.* 53 *ad Antonium*, M.P.L., Vol. 3, Col. 770.
38. *Ep.* 59 *ad Cornelium*.

the Roman Pontiff has succeeded to Peter's prerogatives. St. Firmilian, who was Cyprian's colleague in the East in the baptismal controversy, clearly states that Stephen, the bishop of Rome, was the foundation of the Church by virtue of the fact that he was the successor of Peter.[39]

A classical Fourth Century testimony to the primacy of the bishop of Rome is found in a letter of St. Jerome. While in the East, St. Jerome was accused of heresy by certain Oriental monks. In order to discover the correct teaching on the controverted point, he wrote to Pope Damasus at Rome. It is in this letter that there is contained his most famous reference to the primacy of the Roman Pontiff. He writes:

Therefore have I thought that I ought to consult the Chair of Peter, and the faith that was commended by the mouth of the apostle. . . . From a priest a victim asks safety; from a shepherd a sheep asks protection. Envy avaunt; away with the pride of the topmost dignity of Rome; I speak with the Fisherman's Successor, and the disciple of the cross. Following no chief but Christ, I am joined in communion with your holiness, that is, with the Chair of Peter. Upon that Rock I know that the Church is built.[40]

In this passage, Jerome bases the authority of the bishop of Rome on the fact that he is the successor of St. Peter who was the shepherd of the Flock of Christ and the foundation stone of His Church.

A last indication—space permits no more—of the primacy of the bishop of Rome over the bishops of the world—even the patriarch of Constantinople—is the action of St. Celestine, the bishop of Rome, against Nestorius, patriarch of Constantinople, at the General Council of Ephesus, held in 431 A.D. Nestorius had been preaching heretical doctrines and this Council was convoked to assert the orthodox teaching of the Church against him. Celestine did not attend in person, but instructed his representative, St. Cyril of Alexandria, on what

39. Inter Ep. S Cypriani *Ep.* 75.
40. *Ep.* 15 *ad Damasum,* M.P.L., Vol. 22, Col. 355.

THE MARK OF APOSTOLICITY

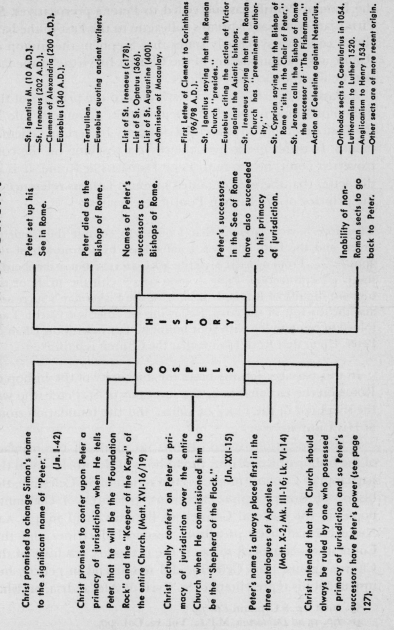

Christ promised to change Simon's name to the significant name of "Peter." (Jn. 1-42)

Christ promises to confer upon Peter a primacy of jurisdiction when He tells Peter that he will be the "Foundation Rock" and the "Keeper of the Keys" of the entire Church. (Matt. XVI-16/19)

Christ actually confers on Peter a primacy of jurisdiction over the entire Church when He commissioned him to be the "Shepherd of the Flock." (Jn. XXI-15)

Peter's name is always placed first in the three catalogues of Apostles.
(Matt. X-2; Mk. III-16; Lk. VI-14)

Christ intended that the Church should always be ruled by one who possessed a primacy of jurisdiction and so Peter's successors have Peter's power (see page 127).

GOSPELS — HISTORY

Peter set up his See in Rome.
—St. Ignatius M. (10 A.D.).
—St. Irenaeus (202 A.D.).
—Clement of Alexandria (200 A.D.).
—Eusebius (340 A.D.).

Peter died as the Bishop of Rome.
—Tertullian.
—Eusebius quoting ancient writers.

Names of Peter's successors as Bishops of Rome.
—List of St. Irenaeus (c178).
—List of St. Optatus (366).
—List of St. Augustine (400).
—Admission of Macaulay.

Peter's successors in the See of Rome have also succeeded to his primacy of jurisdiction.
—First Letter of Clement to Corinthians (96/98 A.D.).
—St. Ignatius saying that the Roman Church "presides."
—Eusebius citing the action of Victor against the Asiatic bishops.
—St. Irenaeus saying that the Roman Church has "preeminent authority."
—St. Cyprian saying that the Bishop of Rome "sits in the Chair of Peter."
—St. Jerome calls the Bishop of Rome the successor of "The Fisherman."
—Action of Celestine against Nestorius.

Inability of non-Roman sects to go back to Peter.
—Orthodox sects to Caerularius in 1054.
—Lutheranism to Luther 1520.
—Anglicanism to Henry 1534.
—Other sects are of more recent origin.

action he wanted the Council to take against Nestorius. It is difficult to find a clearer assertion of the primacy of jurisdiction over the bishops of the rest of the world than is contained in this letter of instruction to Cyril. It reads as follows:

Wherefore, having added to you the authority of our Throne, and using with power our Authority of place, you will exact with rigorous firmness this definite sentence, that either within ten days, counting from the day of this admonition, he shall anathematize, by a confession under his own hand, this wicked assertion of his, and shall give assurance that he will hold, concerning the generation of the Christ and our God, the same faith as the Church of the Romans, and of your Holiness, and the religion the world holds; or if he will not do this, your Holiness, having at once provided for this church [Constantinople], will let him know that he is in every way removed from our Body.[41]

Nestorius refused to recant his errors and was excommunicated.

The oldest non-literary evidence which points to the acceptance by the other bishops of the world of the primacy of the Roman See is the famous inscription of Abercius, a bishop of Hieropolis of Phrygia Salutaris, Asia Minor. The inscription is cut into a pillar which was the tombstone of the grave of Abercius. It is possible that it was made as early as 165 A.D. but certainly not later than 220 A.D. It was found by Ramsay in 1883 and is now preserved in the Lateran Museum in Rome. De Rossi and other first-rate scholars found it an easy task to refute those who attempted to weaken the probative force of this inscription.

After the Fifth Century, evidence indicating the primacy of jurisdiction of the Roman Pontiff is abundant.

There can be no reasonable doubt that the bishop of Rome, by virtue of the fact that he was the successor of St. Peter, not only regarded himself as possessing a primacy of jurisdiction

41. *Ep. ad Cyrillum in Concilium Ephesinum apvd Mansi-Concilia,* T. IV, Col. 1011.

over all the bishops and patriarchs of the Church, but the bishops themselves regarded him as the Foundation Stone of the Church and the Chief Shepherd of the Flock of Christ.

Once it has been proved that the Roman Church possesses the mark of apostolicity, it follows that no other church can possess it, for Christ founded but one Church.[42] However, one need not be satisfied with this negative approach to the question. It can be proved positively that non-Roman churches are not apostolic simply by naming their founders. If they were not founded on Peter, they are not apostolic. The following table shows the founders of the different non-Roman sects:

Name	Founder	Date	Place
Orthodox churches	Michael Caerularius	1054	Constantinople
Lutheranism	Martin Luther	1520	Germany
Anglicanism	King Henry VIII	1534	England
Mennonite sects	Menno Simons	1550	Switzerland
Presbyterianism	Calvin & Knox	1560	Switz. & Scotland
Congregationalism	Robert Brown	1582	Holland
Baptist sects	John Smyth	1606	Amsterdam, Holland
Society of Friends	George Fox	1624	England
Methodism	John Wesley	1744	England
Unitarianism	Theophilos Lindsay	1774	London, England
Mormonism	Joseph Smith	1830	Fayette, N. J., U.S.A.
Adventist sects	William Miller	1840	Boston, Mass., U.S.A.
Salvation Army	William Booth	1865	London, England
Christian Scientists	Mary Baker Eddy	1879	Boston, Mass., U.S.A.

42. Clement of Alexandria, *Paedagogus* Bk. 1. 6. 41. Tertullian, *De Baptismo* Ch. 15.

Not a single one of these sects can prove that it goes back to the person of Peter, and, therefore, none of them possesses the mark of apostolicity by which Christ wished His Church to be identified.

XVI

The Mark of Universality

IN THIS CHAPTER is discussed the second mark which Christ impressed upon His Church to distinguish it from false churches. The most objective way to delineate this mark is to pay close attention to the manner in which Christ refers to it, to permit Christ to speak for Himself. This mark is that of universality of time and place and several observations attest to its existence in the Gospels.

Christ stated that His doctrines would be taught to all nations. Since He made this statement without qualifications as to time, He meant that they would be taught in all ages. It is impossible to preach to all nations without preaching in all ages, for new nations are continuously appearing on the face of the earth. This two-fold universality of time and place is contained in these passages which record the words of Christ:

And he said to them, "Go into the whole world and preach the gospel to every creature. He who believes and is baptized shall be saved, but he who does not believe shall be condemned." [Mark 16:15–16]

And Jesus drew near and spoke to them saying, "All power in heaven and on earth has been given to me. Go, therefore, and make disciples of all nations, baptizing them in the name of the Father, and of the Son, and of the Holy Spirit, teaching them to observe all that I have commanded you; and behold, I am with you all days, even unto the consummation of the world." [Matt. 28:18–20]

"And the gospel of the kingdom shall be preached in the whole world, for a witness to all nations." [Matt. 24:14]

"Thus it is written; and thus the Christ should suffer, and should rise again from the dead on the third day; and that repentance and remission of sins should be preached in his name to all nations, beginning from Jerusalem." [Luke 24:46]

"For they will deliver you up to councils, and you will be beaten in synagogues, and you will stand up before governors and kings for my sake, and for a witness to them. And the gospel must first be preached to all the nations." [Mark 13:9]

"Amen I say to you, wherever in the whole world this gospel is preached, this also that she has done shall be told in memory of her." [Matt. 26:13]

The mark of universality which these passages contain is drawn out in this way. These references state that Christ wished His doctrines to be taught to all nations in all ages. In a previous chapter, it was proved that Christ expressly entrusted the task of diffusing His doctrines to His Church. Now, for Christ's Church to teach all nations in all ages, it must be found in all nations and ages, and, therefore, must have a universality of time and place.

Christ, as to His human nature, was a member of the Semitic race. Now, when the Jewish peoples wished to emphasize a point in conversation or in writing, they could first state it positively and then negatively. In the passages which were quoted concerning the mark of universality, Christ stated His point positively. There are passages in the Gospels in which He states the same point negatively. For instance:

"For whoever is ashamed of me and my words, of him will the Son of Man be ashamed when he comes in his glory." [Luke 9:26]

"And whatever town you enter . . . say to them, 'The kingdom of God is at hand to you.' But whatever town you enter and they do not receive you—go out into its streets and say, 'Even the dust from your town that cleaves to us we shake off against you; yet know this, that the kingdom of God is at hand.' I say to you, that it will be more tolerable for Sodom in that day than for that town. . . . He who hears you, hears me; and he who rejects you, rejects me; and he who rejects me, rejects him who sent me." [Luke 10:8–16]

"The kingdom of heaven is like a king who made a marriage feast for his son. And he sent his servants to call those invited to the marriage feast, but they would not come. Again he sent out other servants . . . but they made light of it. . . . But when the king heard of it, he was angry; and he sent his armies and destroyed those murderers, and burnt their city. Then he said to his servants, 'The marriage feast indeed is ready, but those who were invited were not worthy; go therefore to the crossroads, and invite to the marriage feast whomever you shall find.' And his servants went out into the roads, and gathered all whom they found, both good and bad." [Matt. 22:2–10]

The first two passages show Christ pronouncing penalties against anyone who refuses to accept His teaching. By this He shows that His doctrines are to be universally diffused. The parable contained in the last passage figuratively shows that God makes it obligatory for all people to belong to Christ's Church.

The conclusion to these few observations is that Christ founded a Church with the mark of universality. To distinguish His Church from false churches, Christ intended that it should be spread among all nations in all ages. Its teaching sphere would be the entire world for it would have a universality of place; it must have been teaching since the time of Christ for it was to exhibit a universality of time. If a given church in the world today does not exhibit this two-fold universality, then it cannot lay claim to this mark which Christ intended should distinguish His Church from false churches.

The Identification of the Church with the Mark of Universality

According to the Will of Christ, it is impossible to dissociate the two parts of the mark of universality. To possess this mark, a church must be universal in time and in place. It is evident that an historical inquiry must be made to discover which Church possesses this characteristic.

The first indication of the universality of Christ's Church is found in the writing of the two pagan Latin authors, Tacitus (c. 55–120) and Pliny (c. 61–113). Their testimonies are not conclusive, but they are a valuable prelude to the clear testimonies of later writers.

In describing the persecution of the Christians in Rome under the Emperor Nero (64–69), Tacitus had occasion to mention the number of persons involved. He wrote as follows:

Nero falsely accused and punished with the most fearful tortures the persons commonly called Christians, who were hated for their wicked practices. Christus, the founder of that name, was put to death as a criminal by Pontius Pilate in the reign of Tiberius, but the pernicious superstition repressed for a time, broke out again not only throughout Judea, where the mischief originated, but also in the city of Rome. . . . Accordingly, first those were seized who confessed, next on their information, a vast multitude was convicted, not so much in the charge of burning the city as of hating the human race.[1]

In this passage, Tacitus not only states that within three decades after the death of Christ, Christianity had spread from

1. *Annales* Bk. XX. 44; trans. by John Jackson in Loeb Classical Library (London, Heinemann). Used with permission of Harvard University Press.

Judea to Rome, but also that it had taken root in Rome for a "vast multitude" of Christians were convicted. Now if a "vast multitude" were convicted, it is not too much to presume that an even larger multitude escaped detection.

Pliny the Younger was sent to be the Roman legate to the province of Bithynia in Asia Minor. At this time Christianity was a proscribed religion, making it unlawful for anyone to belong to it. When Pliny arrived in Bithynia, he found so many Christians there that the enforcement of the imperial decrees against them presented a real problem. Being at a loss as to how to cope with the situation, he sent a letter to the Emperor Trajan asking his advice. This letter was written about 108–110 A.D. and a copy of it is extant today. In it, Pliny clearly refers to the number of Christians in Bithynia. In asking advice on this matter, he writes:

This seems a matter for prompt consideration, especially since so many people were endangered. Many of all ages, and both sexes are put in peril of their lives by their accusers. And the process will go on for the contagion of this supersition [i.e., Christianity] has spread not merely through the towns, but into villages and farms. . . .[2]

In his reply to Pliny, Emperor Trajan merely interprets the existing imperial decrees against Christians. This implies a great deal. Pagan Rome tolerated all religions so long as they did not offer a threat to her supremacy. Evidence is yearly uncovered proving that many Eastern cults found their way to the capital city where their devotees built temples and maintained cemeteries. The fact that there was definite anti-Christian imperial legislation[3] in the last half of the First Century shows that the pagan officials thought that Christianity was

2. *Letters* Bk. X, Ep. 96, ad Trajanum, trans. by Melmoth-Hutchinson, in Loeb Classical Library (London; Heinemann, 1924). Used with permission of Harvard University Press.

3. We refer to the sweeping decree of Nero (64–69) mentioned by Tertullian in *Ad Nationes* II. 7.

spreading too rapidly not to threaten the established pagan religion. Celsus in a vicious diatribe entitled *The True Word* (c. 178) betrays his fear that the universal character of the Church is already a definite threat to the national pagan religions of the Empire. Renan, a foe of Christianity, likened the speed of this spread before the year 100 A.D. to a flash of lightning which almost simultaneously lighted up the three peninsulas of Asia Minor, Greece and Italy.

The importance of Pliny's letter is emphasized when one considers the geographical position of Bithynia. It was situated in north-western Asia Minor. It was about midway between Judea and Rome where Tacitus said Christianity was already established. This observation shows how Pliny's testimony supplements that of Tacitus and so prepares the way for the explicit testimony which will now be examined.

The first explicit evidence in extant literature on the universality of the Church appears in the letter of St. Ignatius of Antioch to the Smyrneans, written about 107 A.D. The force of Ignatius' testimony is brought out in this way: Ignatius wrote in Greek. Now, the Greek language does not use the article "the" indiscriminately. It is used only to denote a definite object. The Greek word "katholikos" is a common adjective meaning "universal" or "that which is found everywhere." But when the article "the" and the adjective "katholikos" are combined with a noun, a technical and proper name is coined which refers to a definite object. Thus, St. Ignatius makes this combination in coining a proper name for Christ's Church. This is what he writes:

Wherever the bishop appears, there let the people be; as wherever Jesus Christ is, there is the Catholic Church.[4]

The name by which Ignatius called Christ's Church is not found in the Gospels and so he cannot be said to be merely

4. *Ad Smyrnaeos* ch. 8, trans. by Walsh in *Apostolic Fathers,* "Fathers of the Church Series" (New York; Cima, 1947), Vol. I.

repeating a name which he found there. He used this name because it represented the most striking characteristic of Christ's Church as he knew it. By calling this Church the "Universal" or the "Catholic" Church, he knew that by this name it would be distinguished from all other churches. St. Ignatius' testimony concerning the universality of Christ's Church is important for it shows that already, in the year 107 A.D., this Church had sufficiently spread to be known by the technical name of the "Universal" Church.[5]

The technical name which St. Ignatius used to designate Christ's Church soon became embedded in Christian speech and writing. The extant writing known as the *Martyrdom of St. Polycarp*,[6] written shortly after 155 A.D., gives evidence of this. In the introduction, we read:

The Church of God dwelling as a pilgrim at Smyrna to the Church of God in pilgrimage at Philomelium and to all the congregations of the Holy and Catholic Church in every place.

Again in the eighth chapter:

When finally he concluded his prayer, after remembering all who had at any time come his way—small folk and great folk, distinguished and undistinguished, and the whole Catholic Church throughout the world—the time for departure came.

Then in the sixteenth chapter:

Polycarp certainly was one of the elect, an apostolic and prophetic teacher among our contemporaries and bishop of the Catholic Church in Smyrna.

5. For a discussion of the term "catholic" as found in the epistle of St. Ignatius to the Smyrneans and the *Martyrdom of St. Polycarp*, read the article of J. C. Fenton on the Catholicity of the Church in the *American Ecclesiastical Review*, Vol. CXVII, No. 4 (October, 1947).

6. *Martyrdom of St. Polycarp*, trans. by Glimm in "Fathers of the Church" (New York; Cima, 1947). Used with the permission of Ludwig Schopp.

Finally in the nineteenth chapter:

He rejoices with the Apostles and all the just saints and is glorifying God, the Father Almighty, and blessing our Lord Jesus Christ, the Savior of our souls, the helmsman of our bodies, the shepherd of the Catholic Church throughout the world.

The testimonies of St. Ignatius and of the *Martyrdom of St. Polycarp* are cogent, but it was left to St. Irenaeus of Lyons (c. 130–202) to enumerate the different countries to which Christ's Church had spread. The trustworthiness of Irenaeus' testimony was known even in ancient times. On the universality of the Church he writes:

As I have already observed, the Church having received this preaching and this faith, although scattered throughout the world, yet as if occupying one house carefully preserves it. . . . For the churches which have been planted in Germany do not believe or hand down anything different, nor do those in Spain, nor do those in Gaul, nor do those in the East, nor do those in Egypt, nor do those in Libya, nor do those which have been established in the central regions of the world.[7]

To appreciate fully the force of this testimony, the student should check the countries which Irenaeus mentions on a map of the ancient world. He will notice that Christ's Church had spread to every principal geographical division of the ancient world.

Having shown that there is explicit evidence that the Church possessed a universality of place as early as the Second Century, the task is now to show that it did not lose it in the succeeding centuries.

In the closing years of the Second Century, Tertullian of Carthage (c. 160–220) had occasion to refer to the great num-

7. *Adversus Haereses*, Bk. I. 10. 2; M.P.G., Vol. 7, Col. 552. Cf. also *Adversus Haereses* Bk. II. 9. 1; M.P.G., Vol. 7, Col. 734.

ber of Christians in the Roman Empire. The reference in his *Apologeticum* has become a classic and it reads as follows:

If we desired, indeed, to act the part of open enemies, not merely of secret avengers, would there be any lacking of strength whether of numbers or resources? . . . We are but of yesterday and we have filled every place among you—cities, islands, fortresses, towns, market-places, the very camp, tribes, companies, palace, senate, forum . . . we have left nothing but the temples of your idols. . . . For now it is the immense number of Christians which make your enemies so few . . . almost all the inhabitants of your various cities being followers of Christ.[8]

Toward the middle of the Third Century, Origen of Alexandria (c. 185–254) wrote his famous apology against Celsus. This writing has a slightly different point of view from Tertullian's *Apologeticum*, but it contains an equally explicit reference to the widespread character of the Church of Christ. Origen writes:

And who will not be filled with wonder, when he goes back in thought to Him who then taught and said, "This Gospel shall be preached throughout the whole world. . . ." and beholds in accordance with these words, the Gospel of Jesus Christ, preached in the whole world under heaven to Greeks and barbarians alike? For the word, spoken with power, has gained mastery over men of all sorts of nature and it is impossible to find any race of men which has escaped the teaching of Jesus.[9]

Space does not permit the multiplication of quotations from the writings of ancient authors. Testimony from an Eastern and Western writer will conclude the evidence for the universality of Christ's Church in the first five centuries of this Era.

8. *Apologeticum*, Ch. 37; M.P.L., Vol. I, Col. 462.
9. *Contra Celsum* Bk. II. 13; M.P.G., Vol. II, Col. 820.

One of the Eastern writers who has given evidence on this subject is St. Cyril of Jerusalem (c. 313–386). He leaves no doubt as to the name by which Christ's Church was known in his day when he writes:

The Church is Catholic because she is spread throughout the whole world, that is, from one end to the other; also because she universally and without ceasing teaches all the doctrines which mankind must learn . . . ; furthermore, because she directs all mankind, rulers and subjects, the educated and the unlettered, to the worship and reverence of God.[10]

The Fifth Century witness to the universality of Christ's Church is St. Augustine. It is impossible to mistake the import of this passage from one of his writings:

However, we must distinguish between the case of those who unwittingly join the ranks of heretics, under the impression that they are entering the true Church of Christ, and those who know that there is no other Catholic Church save that which according to the promise, is spread abroad throughout the whole world and extends even to the utmost limits of the earth.[11]

If one would examine the writings of the authors of the first five centuries of Christianity, he would find literally scores of quotations and proofs that Christ's Church was spread throughout the known world. It possessed a universality of place. There is no need to quote primary sources to span the years from the Fifth Century to the present day. Reliable historical works contain the information which is sought; for instance, Professor Emerton, of Harvard University, has a very pointed paragraph on this subject. He writes:

. . . more than this, religion in the Eleventh Century meant only the creed and the forms of the Roman Catholic Church. Whatever

10. *Catechesis* XVIII. 23; M.P.G., Vol. 33, Col. 1048.
11. *Contra Cresconium Donatistam* IV. 5; M.P.L., Vol. 43, Col. 549.

varied from these carried its own condemnation as more or less well-defined heresy. On this point there was not real difference of opinion. The bold defiances of enlightened minds in the Fourteenth Century in defense of frankly heretical ideas was utterly foreign to the Eleventh.[12]

Concerning the universality of the Catholic Church at the beginning of modern times, the distinguished historian, Carlton J. H. Hayes, writes:

For centuries prior to the Sixteenth, the Catholic Church had occupied a position in most European countries which no religious organization holds today. Every child of Christian parents was born into the Church almost as literally as he was born into the state; every professed Christian was expected to conform, at least outwardly, to the doctrines and observances of the Church.[13]

The evidence which has been brought forth is sufficient to warrant the conclusion that Christ's Church has always enjoyed a universality of place. To be sure, this does not mean that every person who lived during this time was a member of this Church. To be universal, it is enough that this Church should have exercised its teaching office in every part of the civilized world. This it did. Because of its universality, in ancient times Christ's Church was known as the "Catholic" Church. This Church has continued to exist to the present day and, even today, it is known as the "Catholic" Church. Today this name is not a misnomer, for today, as in ancient times, it has a universality of place.

The "Catholic" Church also has a universality of time.

12. Emerton, *The Correspondence of Gregory VII; Select Letters from the Registrum* (New York; Columbia University Press, 1932), p. ix.

13. Hayes, *A Political and Cultural History of Modern Europe* (New York; Macmillan, 1937), I, 136.

When ancient writers speak of the "Catholic" Church, they[14] identify it as that Church whose supreme ruler was the bishop of Rome. There is explicit evidence for this. Now in discussing the mark of apostolicity, it was proved that the bishop of Rome is the direct successor of St. Peter. That line of successors has not been broken from the time of Peter to the present day. Since the "Catholic" Church has always been ruled by the bishop of Rome, it follows that this Church has a universality of time. Since the time of Christ the existence of this Church has never been interrupted.

The non-Roman sects do not possess the two-fold universality of time and place which is the characteristic of Christ's Church. They do not possess a universality of time, because, as has already been proved, they have not existed from the time of Christ. The table on page 167 shows that they did not come into existence until many centuries after Christ.

None of the non-Roman sects possesses a universality of place. It is impossible to name one of them whose teaching influence is spread all over the world. Anglicanism is confined chiefly to English-speaking countries; Lutheranism is found principally among the Teutonic races; the Orthodox Church has always been identified with the Slavic peoples and peoples of the Near East. The teaching influence of the smaller non-Roman sects is even more localized than the major groups mentioned, and they have even less right to claim a universality of place.

The conclusion drawn from this discussion is that the Roman Church is the only Church which possesses the universality of time and place which Christ wished His Church to have to distinguish it from all false teaching agencies.

14. St. Cyprian *Epistula 48 ad Cornelium* M.P.L., Vol. 4, Col. 341–42; St. Optatus *De Schismate Donatistarum* Bk. II. 1–6; M.P.L., Vol. II, Col. 941–58; St. Ambrose *De Exessu Fratris Sui Satyri* 47 M.P.L., Vol. 16, Col. 1306; St. Augustine *Contra Donatistas:* De Unitate Ecclesiae, M.P.L., Vol. 43, Col. 389–446, and *Contra Epistolam Manichei Fundamenti* VIII. 5; M.P.L., Vol. 42, Col. 178–79.

THE MARK OF UNIVERSALITY

Christ instructed the Apostles to teach the Gospel "to the whole of creation." (Mk. XVI-15)

Christ told the Apostles to go out and "make disciples of all nations." (Matt. XXVIII-18)

Christ said that "all nations must hear the truth." (Matt. XXIV-14)

Christ said that "repentance and the remission of sin must be preached to all nations beginning at Jerusalem." (Lk. XXIV-46)

Christ warned that in spite of persecution the Gospel must be preached to all nations. (Mk. XIII-9)

Christ predicted that as the Gospel was diffused all over the world so would the account of Magdalene's act of kindness be made known. (Matt. XXVI-13)

Christ warned that He will be ashamed of anyone who is ashamed of Him and His teaching. (Lk. IX-26)

Under the figure of the marriage feast Christ showed that all men have the obligation to accept the benefits which He would make available to them through His Church. (Matt. XXII-2/10)

Since Christ commissioned only His Church to teach all nations, it follows that the influence of this Church must be felt all over the world.

Since Christ commissioned His Church to teach all nations, it follows that it must exercise its teaching office in all ages for new nations are continuously appearing on the earth.

G O S P E L S   H I S T O R Y

Tacitus and Pliny remark with what speed Christianity spread in the First Century.

St. Ignatius of Antioch (107 A.D.) calls the Church "Catholic" because its most striking characteristic is that it is found everywhere.

The Martyrdom of St. Polycarp shows that the name "Catholic" is an accepted technical term as early as the middle of the Second Century.

St. Irenaeus enumerates the countries to which the Church has spread in his time. They are in every quarter of the then known world.

Tertullian shows how the Church has spread within the Roman Empire.

Origen says that Christ's Gospel is "preached in the whole world under heaven to Greeks and barbarians alike."

St. Cyril says that the Church is called "Catholic" because her teaching influence has reached all mankind.

St. Augustine says the "Catholic" Church is spread throughout the whole world.

Emerton identifies religion with Catholicism in the Eleventh Century.

Non-Catholic sects do not have universality of time for they were founded centuries after Christ.

Non-Catholic sects do not have universality of place for Orthodox sects are among the Slavs, Lutheranism among Teutons, and Anglicanism among English.

XVII

The Mark of Unity

ALTHOUGH ONE MARK would be sufficient to distinguish Christ's Church from churches not founded by Him, the student should not neglect to investigate the possibility that Christ impressed more than one mark on His Church. The distinction which one mark proves to exist would become overwhelming if it could be shown that the Church has several identifying marks.

The next mark which Christ impressed upon His Church is Unity. It is two-fold, embracing a unity of doctrine and a unity of government.

No less than sixteen times do the Evangelists use the term "Gospel"[1] to denote the substance of the teachings of Christ. Now the striking feature about the use of this term is that in every instance it is qualified by adjectives and demonstratives to read "the Gospel" or "this Gospel." This shows that whenever Christ speaks of "the Gospel," He is not referring to some indefinite, nondescript set of doctrines, but to one very specific group of teachings. This group of teachings He makes His own for He uses the terms "the Gospel" and "My words" synonymously, as can be seen from the texts.

But he told them, "I must preach the gospel of God's kingdom to other cities too; it is for this that I was sent." [Luke 4:43]

1. For a discussion of the term "Gospel" as used in the New Testament cf. F. Prat. S.J., *The Theology of St. Paul,* trans. by Stoddard (London; Burns, Oates and Washbourne Ltd., 1942), II, 396–400.

"Amen, amen, I say to you, he who hears my word, and believes him who sent me, has life everlasting, and does not come to judgment, but has passed from death to life." [John 5:24]

"For whoever is ashamed of me and my words in this adulterous and sinful generation, of him will the Son of Man also be ashamed when he comes with the holy angels in the glory of his Father." [Mark 8:38]

It can be further demonstrated that the term "the Gospel" means the body of doctrine which Christ came to teach. A comparison of Matthew 28:19–20 with its parallel, Mark 16:15, proves this. Notice how Christ's teachings and "the Gospel" are used synonymously.

"All power in heaven and on earth has been given to me. Go, and make disciples of all nations, baptizing them in the name of the Father, and of the Son, and of the Holy Spirit, teaching them to observe all that I have commanded you." [Matt. 28:20]

"Go into the whole world and preach the gospel to every creature. He who believes and is baptized shall be saved, but he who does not believe shall be condemned." [Mark 16:15]

When Christ commissioned His Apostles and His Church to teach in His stead, He intended that their subject matter should be "the Gospel" or His group of doctrines. Since He did not authorize any addition, subtraction or substitution in this body of doctrines which they were to teach, it follows that His Church was to be characterized by the fact that it transmits to all men one single group of teachings and, therefore, has an established set of doctrines.

Christ not only intended that His Church should teach one unchanging body of doctrine, but He also intended that it should itself be a unified group. This is shown by the fact that Christ assigned to His Church only one government whose authority extended to all its members. This unified government was set up when Christ conferred upon only one person a primacy of jurisdiction. Therefore, the texts which show that Christ conferred on Peter a primacy of jurisdiction, of their very nature, show that Christ set up a Church with a unified government. This observation is fundamental, and it makes clear and easy the interpretation of the other passages in the Gospels which touch upon the structure of Christ's Church. Christ was referring to the unity of government which His Church was to have when He said:

"And I will give to thee the keys to the kingdom of heaven; and whatever thou shalt bind on earth shall be bound in heaven, and whatever thou shall loose on earth shall be loosed in heaven." [Matt. 16:19]

"And other sheep I have that are not of this fold. Them also I must bring, and they shall hear my voice, and there shall be one fold and one shepherd." [John 10:16]

Three times did Christ use the term "church" to designate His group of followers on earth and, in each case, He spoke in the singular number. The terms which Christ used most commonly as synonyms for His Church are "the kingdom of God" and "the kingdom of heaven." He so qualified them that they can only refer to His Church as it sojourns on earth. About thirty-five times Christ used these terms to mean His Church and in each case they are used in the singular, thus proving that Christ founded only one Church on earth.

Several of the parables of Christ shed light on the unity with which Christ's Church was endowed. One of these parables is that in which Christ compared His Church to a grain of mustard seed. Mustard seed is the smallest of seeds, but when it grows up it becomes the largest of herbs, so that the birds come and settle on its branches. The other is the one in which Christ compared His Church to a dragnet which catches all types of fishes. In both of these parables the allusion to the unity of the Church is apparent.

The reasons which have been outlined in this chapter show that Christ intended His Church to exhibit a two-fold unity. It was to be distinguished from other churches by a unity of doctrine and a unity of government.

The Identification of the Church with the Mark of Unity

The mark of unity which Christ impressed upon His Church has a two-fold character. Christ wished His Church to stand out by the fact that it taught one body of doctrine and that it was organized with one government.

The first part of the inquiry will aim to discover which Church has a unity of doctrine. There is much evidence in extant ancient ecclesiastical literature to show that from the very beginning of Christianity, there existed numerous sects which propagated doctrines contrary to the teachings of the Church. One of the most influential of these groups was the Gnostics.[2] But soon there appeared writers who refuted the heterodox doctrines of these Gnostics. The argument which these Christian writers used was brilliantly simple and proved to be effective, for Gnosticism waned and eventually disappeared. The Christian writers said that since truth is absolute, it cannot change. Since Christ's doctrines are true, they are immutable. The doctrines of the Gnostics could not be true because they were always changing. St. Irenaeus was especially emphatic in pointing out that the touchstone of the truth of a doctrine is its conformity with primitive tradition.[3] If it had not changed from the beginning, then it was true. This was

2. Gnostics claimed to have a superior and mystical revelation over and above the original deposit of faith.

3. *Adversus Haereses* Bk. II. 9. 1; and Bk. III. 12. 8.

but another way of stating that only the True Church teaches a unified body of doctrine.

The writers of the ante-Nicene Era did not leave this discussion on the immutability of Christ's doctrines in the speculative state. They showed that, as a matter of fact, there was a Church which was one in Doctrine. They said:

Hegesippus has left a complete record of his own opinion in five treatises which has come down to us. In them he explains how when traveling as far as Rome, he mingled with many bishops, and that he found the same doctrine among them all.[4]

One of the clearest quotations in favor of the unity of doctrine of Christ's Church in all ante-Nicene literature is this one, found in the *Adversus Haereses* of St. Irenaeus. It reads as follows:

As I have already observed, the Church having received this preaching and this faith, although scattered throughout the world carefully preserves it. She also believes these points of doctrine just as if she had but one soul and one and the same heart, and proclaims and teaches them and hands them down with perfect harmony as if she possessed but one mouth. . . . For the faith being ever one and the same, neither does one who is able at great length to discourse regarding it, make any additions to it, nor does one who can say but little, diminish it.[5]

Tertullian was another writer who insisted that the conformity of a doctrine with primitive tradition be the test of its truth.

He points this out in one of his better-known works:

But if there be any heresies which are bold enough to plant themselves in the midst of the apostolic age, that they may seem to have

4. *H.E.* Bk. IV. 22. 1; Loeb Edition, Vol. I, p. 375.
5. *Adversus Haereses* Bk. I. 10. 2; M.P.G., Vol. 7, Col. 552.

been handed down from the apostles, because they existed in the time of the apostles, we can say; let them produce the original records of their churches; let them unfold the roll of their bishops, running down in due succession from the beginning in such a manner that (that first bishop of theirs) bishop shall be able to show for his ordainer and predecessor some one of the apostles or of apostolic men. . . .[6]

Tertullian goes on to speak of the doctrine:

For their very doctrine, after comparison with that of the apostles, will declare, by its own diversity and contrariety, that it has for its author neither an apostle nor an apostolic man.

In other references, the writers who were quoted above, and many more,[7] point out that the Church which teaches a uniform body of doctrine is either the Church whose supreme ruler is the bishop of Rome or the Church which is known as the "Catholic" Church. It was previously proved that these are one and the same Church.

There is a more direct method than the one just completed which arrives at the conclusion that the Roman Church has always taught a uniform body of doctrine. Its importance lies in the fact that it easily bridges the centuries from ancient to modern times.

The task of imparting articles of faith is greatly facilitated when the articles are summarized in a formula of faith or a creed. In this way they can be easily memorized and retained. Throughout the period of her existence, the Roman Church has, from time to time, drawn up creeds or professions of faith. These creeds do not contain the articles of faith in an exhaustive fashion but they are sufficiently detailed to permit tracing

6. *De Praescriptione Haereticorum* ch. 32; M.P.L., Vol. 2, Col. 44.
7. Irenaeus, *Adv. Haer.* Bk. II. 3. 2; Cyprian, *Epistola* 55 and 76; Tertullian, *De Praescrip. Heret.*, chs. 26 and 30; Tertullian, *Adversus Marcionem* Bk. IV. 4.

the uniformity of the teaching of the Roman Church through the centuries. These are the names and dates of the principal creeds which have been drawn up under the authority of the Roman Church:

Apostles' Creed[8]	2nd Century
Nicene Creed	325 A.D.
Nicene-Constantinopolitan Creed	381 A.D.
Epiphanian Creed	4th Century
Antipriscillian Creed	4th Century
Athanasian Creed	5th Century
Creed of XI Council of Toledo	675 A.D.
Leonine Creed	1053 A.D.
Tridentine Creed	1564 A.D.

On several occasions, the Roman Church has drawn up professions of faith to discover the religious tenets of different groups which wished to be admitted into her membership. One of these professions was drawn up in 1575 for the Greeks; another was drawn up for the Maronites in 1743. In composition these professions are similar to the creeds. A comparison of these creeds and professions of faith with each other shows that the Roman Church has always taught the same articles of faith and, therefore, possesses uniformity of doctrine.

The explanation of the fact that certain doctrines are especially stressed in some creeds and not in others is to be sought in the historical situation which caused the formulation of the creed. In general, a doctrine of faith was defined when that doctrine was impugned. The date of definition is not the date when that doctrine was first taught. A definition merely makes explicit that which was taught implicitly from the beginning.

8. Most of the articles of the Apostles' Creed are contained in the letters of St. Ignatius of Antioch (died c. 107 A.D.), but the earliest evidence of the formulation into a creed is found in the Second Century in the writings of St. Justin M. and St. Irenaeus (*Adv. Haer.* I. 10. 1). The book which contains all the definitions of the doctrines and creeds of the Roman Church is entitled *Enchiridion Symbolorum,* compiled by Denzinger-Bannwart-Umberg-Rahner, 1952.

St. Vincent of Lerins in his *Commonitorium* (434 A.D.) is
followed by John Henry Newman in his *Essay on the Development of Christian Doctrine* (1845) in showing that a certain
development of a doctrine does not militate against its essential unity. A doctrine does not develop in the sense that new
meaning is added to it but in the sense that meaning that was
always there is now unfolded. The truth itself does not grow
but our understanding of it can and does grow. It is only reasonable then that this deeper understanding should be set
down in more expressive terms.

It was just remarked that many times a teaching that had
been held for a long time and which was but mentioned in
passing by previous writers needed a historical situation to
make it burst into the limelight of Christian literature. A situation developed late in the Fourth Century which really threw
into bold relief the mark of the Unity of the Church. The
evidence of this characteristic in ante-Nicene literature is unmistakable but it remained for St. Ambrose (A.D. 333–397) to
unfold it completely and to set it down with precision. A ter-
rible schism had developed in the important See of Antioch.
Ambrose in his writings and especially in his letters[9] reminded
the schismatics that the Church is a definite, organized and
unified society. He struck at the heart of the schism when he
repeated that this unity was insured by the communion of the
bishops throughout the world with the bishop of Rome who
had succeeded to Peter's primacy of authority.[10] It is not without reason that of the 29 doctors of the Church, St. Ambrose,
the intrepid bishop of Milan, should have the added title of
Doctor of the Unity of the Church. And it is not surprising
that when later writers on this subject quote him intelligently
their works command respect and authority.

It was proved in another discussion that Christ conferred
only upon Peter, from among the Apostles, a primacy of juris-

9. Cf. especially *Letters 11, 13* and *56*.
10. In Psalm 11:30 and *De Paenitentia 33*.

diction. Christ intended that this primacy should remain in the Church throughout the period of its existence. Since the bishop of Rome is the successor of St. Peter and possesses the same jurisdiction which Christ wished Peter to have, it follows that he is the supreme ruler of the universal Church. From the fact that every member of this universal Church is subject to the bishop of Rome, it must be concluded that the Roman Catholic Church possesses the unity of government which Christ impressed upon His Church.

It is the Roman Catholic Church which is justified in laying claim to the two-fold unity of doctrine and government.

The existence in the Roman Catholic Church of several rites does not militate against its unity of doctrine or government. This Church is called "Roman" because its supreme ruler who exercises jurisdiction over Latins and Orientals is the Bishop of Rome. The Orientals[11] believe exactly the same body of doctrine as do the Latins and so there is unity of belief among them. But there is an accidental difference between Latins and Orientals in that the liturgy and certain points of discipline are not the same. This does not constitute an essential difference and, therefore, the unity of the Roman Church is not affected.

The non-Catholic religious groups do not possess a unity of doctrine. Space does not permit the listing of the changes which have taken place in their body of doctrine since they were founded. But Harnack has admitted that:

And when we are reproached with our divisions and told that Protestantism has as many doctrines as heads, we reply, "So it has, but we do not wish it otherwise; on the contrary, we want still more freedom, still greater individuality in utterance and in doctrine.[12]

11. By "Orientals" are meant the members of the Syrian, Maronite, Chaldean, Malabar, Aramaean, Melchite, Coptic and Byzantine Rites. The members number approximately six million.

12. Harnack, *What is Christianity*, trans. by Saunders (New York; G. P. Putnam's Sons, 1901), p. 269.

THE MARK OF UNITY

GOSPELS / HISTORY

Christ's use of the term "The Gospel" in sixteen places shows that He wished His Church to teach but one body of doctrine.

Christ authorized no change in doctrine for He pronounces condemnation against those who refuse to accept "Me and My words." (Mk. VIII-38)

Christ uses the term "church" twice in the Gospels and the term "Kingdom of Heaven" thirty-five times to designate His Church and in each time it is in the singular, thus showing that He wished to found but one church.

Christ endowed but one person with a primacy of jurisdiction, thus proving that His Church would be one in government. (Matt. XVI-16 and Jn. XXI-15)

Christ compared His Church to a sheep-fold which was watched over by one shepherd. He said, "I have other sheep too, which do not belong to this fold; I must bring them in too; they will listen to my voice; so there will be one fold and one shepherd." (Jn. X-16)

Christ indicated the unity of His Church when He compared it to a single tree which gathers all types of birds in its branches (Matt. XII-31) and to a drag-net which encloses all types of fishes. (Matt. XIII-47)

Christ implied that His Church would be one in belief and love when He prayed, "That while thou art in me, I may be in turn in them, and so they may be perfectly made one." (Jn. XVIII-23)

Hegesippus (2nd Century) says that he had found a unanimity of belief among the bishops he had visited in various places.

St. Irenaeus (d. c. 202 A.D.) says that although the Church is scattered throughout the world she teaches as "though she possessed but one mouth."

Tertullian urges that the doctrine of the Church has been the same since it was imparted to her from the beginning.

A comparison of the different creeds and professions of faith shows that the doctrines of the Catholic Church have been the same throughout the centuries.

Since it can be proved that the Catholic Church has always been ruled by a person who possessed a primacy of jurisdiction, it follows that she has always had a unity of government.

St. Cyprian of Carthage wrote a famous treatise entitled "The Unity of the Catholic Church."

There are several hundred different non-Catholic sects in existence today. They are independent of each other thus proving that they do not have unity of government.

Harnack is one of many non-Catholic theologians who admits that the various sects do not teach and profess faith in an unchanging set of doctrines.

There is not a single non-Catholic sect in which all the members must believe the same doctrines.

Since the middle of the Nineteenth Century some Anglicans have proposed a doctrine called the "branch theory." It holds that Christ's Church is one but this unity is a composition of three parts or branches. One branch is called Roman Catholic; another is called Anglican and a third is called Orthodox. The purpose of this theory is quite obvious. It is an attempt to account for the fifteen centuries that intervened between Christ's coming to earth and the appearance of the Church of England in 1534. A second reason flows from the first. It attempts to lay claim to the glorious Christian tradition built up in England before the Sixteenth Century. That tradition was marked by such names as St. Bede the Venerable, Chaucer, St. Thomas à Becket and St. Augustine of Canterbury. To say that Christ's Church first appeared in England in 1534 would leave these two problems unanswered and unanswerable, hence, the excogitation of the "branch theory."[13]

Several things must be said concerning the theory outlined in the above paragraph. The first is that of the three groups which are supposed to make up Christ's Church, the Anglicans who proposed the theory are the only ones who are sympathetic towards it. The second is that there is not a fragment of evidence either in the New Testament or in Tradition which justifies it. Their appeal to the writings of St. Cyprian as an anchor to their arguments is an appeal made entirely out of context. A third observation is that this theory is obviously opposed to the structure of the Church as it was founded by Christ. Christ set up His Church as a perfect society, that is, He left no room for future modification either as re-

13. It is interesting to observe that in point of history, the founders of Anglicanism did not first formulate their theory and then implement it by cutting themselves off from the authority of the Bishop of Rome. Rather, Henry VIII founded this church on the occasion of his failure to obtain a divorce from Catherine of Aragon, and after his break the "branch theory" was devised to attempt to justify his action.

gards its government or its doctrines. The "branch theory" attempts modification on both scores. It would shatter the perfect unity of Christ's Church into many autonomous jurisdictions. It would sanction for belief as true, doctrines which are contrary and even contradictory.[14]

When the founders of Anglicanism set up their church in 1534 as a separate and autonomous entity, they founded a sect essentially different from the Christianity England had known for centuries. Two objects—this includes churches—which are essentially different cannot be variations of the same thing. Sects other than Anglicanism which by implication would set aside the probative force of the mark of unity are merely advocating an extended version of the "branch theory" and their opinions are equally unacceptable.

Non-Catholic sects do not possess a unity of government, either singly or in a group. In no non-Catholic sect is there a person or ruling directory which possesses a primacy of jurisdiction over each and every one of its members.

14. A reliable work showing the diversity of belief among these sects is *Studies in Comparative Religion* (5 volumes) published by the Catholic Truth Society of London.

XVIII

The Mark of Sanctity

THE LAST MARK of the Church is not as explicit in the Gospels as are the first three, but it is sufficiently detailed to be used as a point of distinction between Christ's Church and churches not founded by Him. It is the mark of holiness. In order to lay claim to the principal phases of this mark, a church must exhibit a three-fold sanctity. It must be holy in its Founder, in its doctrine and in its members.

The essence of sanctity is love of God. It is the conforming of one's will to God's will. It is doing what He wishes one to do, and avoiding what He wishes one to avoid. When one maintains his loyalty to God, he is said to be holy. When a doctrine fosters love of God it is holy.

We need not elaborate on the fact that Christ's Church is holy in its Founder. Since Christ proved that He is God, He is Infinite Perfection and Holiness. But one must not think that just because a church calls itself "Christian" it can automatically point to Christ as its Founder. A Christian church has come to mean any organization which claims to teach or believe even a few of the doctrines of Christ. All churches cannot claim to be holy in their founder because we cannot identify any Christian church with the Church founded by Christ.

The true Church must be holy in its doctrine. In formulating this argument, it is not necessary to consider each doctrine separately to show how it fosters sanctity. If the whole body of doctrines can be proved to have been revealed by God, it necessarily follows that it is holy. It will not do to claim to be holy in doctrine when teaching but a few of Christ's doctrines. In order to make this claim it must teach all of them.

A third phase of the mark of sanctity is holiness of members. To possess this characteristic, it is not necessary for each and every one of its members to be of renowned holiness. This is the mark of the Church as an organization, not necessarily an endowment of every member within that organization. For a church to be able to claim to be holy in its members: 1—a notable part of the total number must exhibit ordinary holiness for Christ extended the invitation to holiness and the means of sanctification to all the members of the Church; 2—many within that Church must exhibit a superior holiness for when Christ issued His counsels although He knew that all would not follow them He also knew that all could follow them; 3— at least a few must be noted for their heroic sanctity. While Christ made sanctity a distinguishing mark of His Church, He also said that wicked persons would be found within its ranks. Several parables of Christ make this clear. Let us consider more fully what Christ said concerning the sanctity of the members of His Church.

Christ said that it would be characteristic of the group who would preach His Gospel to have surrendered their personal ambitions and to have put themselves under obedience to a higher authority so that the Gospel might be preached more effectively. He also said that by being celibates, they could more freely preach the Gospel, as these passages show:

"If anyone wishes to come after me, let him deny himself, and take up his cross, and follow me. For he who would save his life will lose it; but he who loses his life for my sake and for the gospel's sake will save it." [Mark 8:34]

"For there are eunuchs who were born so from their mother's womb; and there are eunuchs who were made so by men; and there are eunuchs who have made themselves so for the kingdom of heaven's sake." [Matt. 19:12]

Hence, to embrace a life of obedience and celibacy out of love of God in order to preach the Gospel is an externalization of holiness.

In the next step in the unfolding of this mark of sanctity, Christ presupposes obedience in the individual, but now adds to it voluntary poverty. If anyone would give up earthly possessions so that his love of God would not be obstructed by attachment to them, then certainly this would be an indication of sanctity. In this regard, Christ said:

"Amen I say to you, there is no one who has left house, or brothers, or sisters, or mother, or father, or children, or lands, for my sake and for the gospel's sake, who shall not receive now in the present time a hundredfold as much, houses, and brothers, and sisters, and mothers, and children, and lands—along with persecutions, and in the age to come life everlasting." [Mark 10:29–30]

Jesus said to him, "If thou wilt be perfect, go, sell what thou hast, and give to the poor, and thou shalt have treasure in heaven; and come, follow me." [Matt. 19:21]

The crowning piece of sanctity, according to Christ, was the willingness to suffer ridicule, hatred, physical punishment, and even death,[1] out of the love of God. And when He said that "the servants of the house" would not fare better than "the master of the house" in this matter, He meant that it would be characteristic of His Church to suffer persecution for His sake.

These are the passages which prove this:

"No disciple is above his teacher, nor is the servant above his master. It is enough for the disciple to be like his teacher, and for the

1. Cf. John 15:13.

servant to be like his master. If they have called the master of the house Beelzebub, how much more those of his household." [Matt. 10:24-25]

"If the world hates you, know that it has hated me before you. If you were of the world, the world would love what is its own. But because you are not of the world, but I have chosen you out of the world, therefore the world hates you. . . . If they have persecuted me, they will persecute you also. . . . But all these things they will do to you for my name's sake." [John 15:18-22]

"Blessed are you when men reproach you, and persecute you, and, speaking falsely, say all manner of evil against you, for my sake . . . your reward is great in heaven; for so did they persecute the prophets who were before you." [Matt. 6:11-12]

"These things I have spoken to you that you may not be scandalized. They will expel you from the synagogues. Yes, the hour is coming for everyone who kills you to think that he is offering worship to God. . . ." [John 16:1-2]

To show that the true Church on earth would not be made up of elect alone, Christ compared it to a dragnet which encloses good and bad fishes.[2] He compared it to a wedding feast from which a man was expelled for not having on his wedding garment.[3] But perhaps the best illustration is the parable in which Christ compares His Church to a field in which a man had sown good seed.[4] While he was sleeping, his enemy came and over-sowed it with weed seed. When the grain and weeds sprang up, the master forbade the servants to root out the weeds. He told them to wait until the harvest time to separate the two. These three parables show that in Christ's Church there are good and bad members.

In summarizing the mark of sanctity, it may be said that

2. Matt. 13:47-50.
3. Matt. 22:1-14.
4. Matt. 13:24-30.

Christ indicated that His Church would be characterized by the fact that it would be holy in its Founder, in its doctrine and in its members. In this way, His Church could be distinguished from churches not founded by Him.

The Identification of the Church with the Mark of Sanctity

In discussing the manner in which Christ impressed the mark of sanctity upon His Church, it was noticed that there are several criteria which can be used to prove the existence of this mark. The process which will be followed in this chapter will be to break it down into its principal component parts and then to inquire which present-day Church possesses them. By examining one element of this mark at a time, the student will better appreciate the cogency of the whole.

Christ founded His Church to teach, to rule and to sanctify. It was shown in a previous chapter, that He appointed St. Peter, the Prince of the Apostles, as the first supreme teacher and ruler of His Church. Since it can be proved that the supreme pontiffs of the Catholic Church are the successors of St. Peter, it follows that the teaching and ruling office of the popes was founded by Christ. Christ proved that He was God. Therefore, the Catholic Church is holy in its Founder.

The Catholic Church is holy in its doctrine. In discussing the mark of unity, it was shown that all through her history the Catholic Church has taught but one body of doctrine. We saw that in ancient times such writers as St. Irenaeus (d. 202) and Tertullian (d. c. 220) stressed the fact that while the teachings of the heretical sects were always being revised, the doctrines of the Church had not changed from Apostolic times. But the Apostles taught doctrines directly or indirectly revealed by God. Since God is Infinite Holiness, His doctrines are holy. The Catholic Church to whom these doctrines were confided, then, is holy in doctrine.

The Catholic Church is holy in its members:

Christ said that one indication of superior sanctity was the willingness to forgo one's will and the right to a family in order to be free to preach the Gospel.

There is good evidence[5] that in the first three centuries of the Christian Era, there were large numbers of the clergy of the Roman Church who were celibates and obedient to authority in the exercise of their offices. It is impossible to draw a sharper conclusion from the information which is extant. It cannot be proved that celibacy was obligatory for clerics, but even though it was not strictly obligatory, it was nevertheless widely practiced.

Toward the end of the Third Century, the discipline of the Roman Church concerning celibacy began sharply to change. From this period is dated the first legislation making clerical celibacy obligatory. The earliest extant information on this subject is Canon 33 of the Council of Elvira in Spain, held in the year 295 A.D.[6] This council made it obligatory for the higher ranks of the clergy to be celibates. This legislation was paralleled in the East by similar enactments of the Council of Ancyra (314 A.D.)[7] and the Council of Neo-Caesarea (315 A.D.).[8] Although these councils legislated only for particular districts, their enactments were indicative of the trend of the times. This discipline spread so that it can be safely said that by the year 450 A.D., celibacy of the clergy was the rule in the West. From that time unto the present day, this discipline has been maintained among the clergy of the Latin Rite of the Roman Church.

In certain of the Oriental Rites of the Roman Church, married men have been admitted into the ranks of the clergy, but

5. Tertullian, *De Exhortatione Castitatis* Ch. 13; Origen, *In Lev. Hom.* VI. 6.

6. Hefele, *A History of the Christian Councils,* trans. by Clark (Edinburgh; T. & T. Clark, 1882), I, 150.

7. *Ibid.,* p. 223.

8. *Ibid.,* p. 210.

at no time during the Middle Ages or in modern times was their number large enough to destroy the characteristics of a celibate clergy in this Church.[9] Then, too, it is no difficult task to prove that certain members of the clergy and hierarchy of the Latin Rite did not lead celibate lives. This was especially true during the Renaissance. But, again, this did not constitute a large percentage of the clergy of the time.

There have been clergymen of non-Catholic sects who have lived celibate lives, and whose sincerity cannot be doubted, but their numbers are too small to constitute celibacy as a definite and easily recognizable characteristic of their particular sect.

In conclusion then, it must be said that it is characteristic only of the Roman Church to have a clergy which, in order to preach more freely the Gospel of Christ, have embraced lives of celibacy and obedience. She alone can lay claim to this indication of the mark of sanctity by which Christ wished His Church to be distinguished from all other churches.

It was seen in discussing the mark of sanctity that Christ said that another indication of this mark was voluntary poverty. This virtue might be accompanied by other virtues, such as chastity and obedience. Now when these virtues are practiced out of love of God, it is clearly an indication of sanctity.

In ante-Nicene literature, there is evidence that many people embraced the life of voluntary poverty and chastity in order to follow more easily the way of perfection. St. Justin Martyr, who died in about 167 A.D., attests to the existence of groups of people who practiced these virtues. He writes:

And many, both men and women, who have been Christ's disciples from childhood, remain pure at the age of sixty and seventy; I boast that I can produce such from every race of men.[10]

There are two extant letters falsely ascribed to Clement of

9. The trend today is to make the discipline of the Oriental Rites the same as that of the Latin Rite.

10. Justin M. *I Apology* Ch. 15; cf. also Minucius Felix in *Octavius* Ch. 31.

Rome (died c. 100) but which some scholars for very good reasons pronounce to be a Second Century composition. They contain excellent advice to groups of women consecrated to God found in all the Christian communities of the time and called "the virgins."

An interesting picture dating back to about 250 A.D. was discovered some years ago in the catacombs of Priscilla at Rome. It depicts a young lady receiving from a bishop the veil symbolic of the vow of virginity while she holds in her hand a scroll upon which are written her vows. The Blessed Virgin Mary, model of all virgins, is shown in the same picture. This mural clearly shows that already at this time some of the faithful took public vows of virginity and they constituted a distinct group among the laity. It is also a key to the title "VIRGO" found on many tombs of the catacombs, some of which antedate this painting.[11]

The testimony of Third Century is more abundant and more definite. And it was in the Third Century that monasticism appeared. Egypt is generally looked upon as the cradle of monasticism, but from Egypt it spread throughout the Christian world, and the number who embraced this life was very great. At this time there began to appear monastic rules, thus indicating that this life of perfection was widespread and organized to a certain extent. Monasticism in the early centuries of the Christian Era was characterized by the observance of such virtues as voluntary poverty, chastity, obedience. And the only satisfactory reason which can be assigned for the embracing of this type of life was the love of God.

A great impetus was given to monasticism during the Middle Ages by the founding of the mendicant orders, such as the Dominicans and the Franciscans. The part that these orders played during this time is well known. It is difficult to overestimate their contribution to education and charity.

In modern times, the number of men and women who have entered religious life is very great. Space does not permit the

11. F. Grossi-Condi, S.J., *I Monumenti Cristiani* (Rome, 1923), p. 30.

listing of the religious communities which have been founded in modern times. While taking vows of voluntary poverty, chastity and obedience, they labor in all phases of religious endeavor. They conduct schools for all age levels; they operate hospitals and orphanages; many labor in the mission fields; some are contemplatives.

The monastic life has been widely practiced only in the Roman Catholic Church, and she alone can claim this particular phase of the mark of sanctity which Christ wished His Church to exhibit. While non-Catholic sects have members who have entered upon the religious life in the sense described, it certainly is not characteristic of these sects. Their numbers are not nearly as considerable as those of the Roman Church.

A sign of heroic sanctity is the willingness to suffer, and even die, out of love for Jesus Christ. It is not the punishment itself, but the motive which leads one to endure it, which is the indication of sanctity. And in the evidence which will now be brought forth, the motive which impelled the people to endure persecution was their love for Christ. Every other explanation completely breaks down.

There is ample evidence to prove that the accusations levelled against the early Christians by the pagan authorities were false. Christians were accused of being enemies of the state, of participating in thyestian[12] banquets, atheism, social uselessness, and of other crimes. The apologists of the Second Century—whose writings are extant—showed that these accusations were without foundation and were brought forth only to try to justify the persecutions against the Christians. Perhaps the most famous reply to the pagan accusations in the early centuries is Tertullian's *Apologeticum*. In it he minutely examines and refutes the pagan charges.

Historians enumerate ten general persecutions decreed by

12. This term is derived from the character "Thyestes" in the drama "Agamemnon" of the classical Greek tragedian Aeschylus. Thyestes partakes of a cannibalistic banquet. Fronto of Cirta is quoted by Minucius Felix (*Octavius* Bk. IX. 6) as having made this charge.

the pagan Roman emperors against the followers of Christ up to the year 313 A.D. when the Edict of Milan allowed Christianity the same status as the other religions of the empire. They were the persecutions conducted under Nero (64–69), Domitian (81–96), Hadrian (120–124), Marcus Aurelius (164–176), Septimius Severus (202–211), Maximian (235–237), Decius (249–251), Valerian (257–260), Claudius and Aurelian (269–275), Diocletian (285–305). Besides these general persecutions, there were numerous local persecutions conducted in the provinces by proconsuls and procurators.

The persecutions against Christians were not aimed at any particular group in the Church. They were aimed at anyone who bore the name "Christian,"[13] and this included men, women, and children as well as members of the clergy.[14] When a Christian was tried, he was given an opportunity to apostatize, or to reject his religion. If he did this, the charges against him were dropped. If he refused, he was punished. Many times the penalty was death. It is a hopelessly impossible task to try to count accurately the number of people who were punished during this period for being followers of Christ. In fact, very few reliable writers even venture to estimate the number of persons who were put to death. Judging from the period of time that was spanned by the persecutions, the number who were put to death was very great. Perhaps the greatest authority of modern times on the martyrs was Paul Allard. On this subject he writes:

It is not only true that the witnesses of Christ may be numbered by thousands, but human language is unavailing to describe how many martyrs there have been in towns and provinces.[15]

We then find ourselves faced by the question whether the perseverance of so many thousands of every sex and age who willingly

13. Tertullian, *Apologeticum* Ch. 3.
14. Pliny, *Letters* Bk. X, Ep. 96 ad Trajani.
15. Allard, *Ten Lectures on the Martyrs,* trans. by Cappadelta (New York; Benziger, 1907), p. 136.

bore for the space of three centuries such sufferings, can be explained by merely human strength.[16]

During the Middle Ages, the Christians were persecuted by the Moslems, and one of the most eloquent proofs of the fierceness of these persecutions is the fact that the Church which was highly developed in Asia Minor, Palestine, Egypt, and the whole of North Africa was almost entirely destroyed.

In modern times there have been very few countries in which Christians were not persecuted either formally or informally. They were persecuted in England under Elizabeth and Cromwell; in France during the French Revolution. They have suffered formal persecutions in Mexico, Germany, Russia and Spain. There have been martyrs in such widely separated places as Uganda, and Korea; the Great Lakes region of North America and the South Seas. It is impossible to obtain an accurate number of the martyrs even in modern times, but it is certain that the number is great. As recently as the Spanish Civil War, there were authenticated 968 cases of martyrdom in the Diocese of Barcelona alone.[17] And the martyrs of modern times, like those of ancient times, had the same motivation, namely, the love of God.

Investigation shows that the vast majority of the martyrs are identified with the Roman Church. There have been martyrs who belonged to non-Catholic sects, but they are too few to constitute a characteristic of the sect. It is characteristic only of the Roman Church to have martyrs[18] and so she alone possesses this phase of the mark of sanctity.

The Roman Catholic Church is the sole possessor of all the elements of the mark of sanctity. This fact, coupled with the fact that the Roman Catholic Church alone has saints canon-

16. Allard, *op. cit.*, p. 338.

17. Sanroma, *Martirologio de la Eglesia en la Diocesis de Barcelona durante la Persecucion Religiosa 1936–1939 (Barcelona, 1943).*

18. The Jews have been persecuted throughout history, but for racial and not religious reasons.

THE MARK OF SANCTITY

Sanctity consists in the love of God. Since Christ was God, it follows that the Church He founded is holy in its founder for God is holiness.

Since Christ wished His Church to teach all His doctrines and since this body of doctrine fosters love of God, it follows that Christ's Church must be holy in its doctrine

Christ intended that His Church should be characterized by the sanctity of many of its members.

A. Some would surrender personal ambition to preach the gospel. "It is the man who loses his life for my sake and for the gospel's sake that will save it." (Mk. VIII-34)

B. Some would embrace voluntary poverty in order to serve Christ more easily. "If thou has a mind to be perfect, go home and sell all that belongs to thee and give it to the poor. . . . Then come back and follow me." (Matt. XIX-21)

C. Some would suffer to show their love for Christ. "A disciple is no better than his Master. . . . If they cried Beelzebub at the Master of the house, they will do it much more readily to the members of the household." (Matt. X-24)

G	H
O	I
S	S
P	T
E	O
L	R
S	Y

GOSPELS   HISTORY

Since it was proved that the line of popes can be traced back in unbroken series from the present pope to Peter who received supreme power from Christ, it follows that the Roman Church is holy in its founder.

Since it was proved that the doctrine taught by the Roman Church has been the same since the time of the Apostles who received it from Christ, it follows that this Church is holy in its doctrines.

The Roman Church in Ante-Nicene times had many members of her clergy who were celibates. The Canons of the Council of Elvira (295 A.D.) are the first legislation on this matter. Celibacy was the rule in the West since about 450 A. D.

It is characteristic only of the Roman Church to have many of her members who have bound themselves by the vows of voluntary poverty, chastity, and obedience.

In all the ages of her existence the Roman Church has been the object of persecution. Willingness to suffer for Christ is a sign of sanctity.

Non-Catholic sects have some celibate clergymen, some religious and some who have suffered for their belief but their numbers are insufficient to characterize these as a mark of their sect.

ized according to the rigorous process of Benedict XIV, proves that only this Church possesses this mark as Christ impressed it upon His Church to distinguish it from all others.

The Name of the Church Founded by Christ

Now that the discussion of the marks of the Church has been completed, the stage is set to name the present-day Church which is the one founded by Christ to teach all men what they must do and believe to be saved. Since the name of that Church or another church is not found in the Gospel, one would expect the True Church to be named according to its marks. And this is precisely the case.

Christ founded a Church on Peter. Now since the successors of Peter were proved to be the bishops of Rome, Christ's Church must be called the Roman Church. It was proved that the Roman Church alone possesses the unity of doctrine and government by which Christ wished His Church to be known. And so the Roman Church must also be called One. It was proved that the Roman Church alone possesses all the elements of the mark of sanctity, and so must also be called Holy. It was proved that the Roman Church alone possesses the mark of universality of time and place by which Christ's Church is to be identified. And so the Roman Church alone must also be called universal or Catholic. Gathering all these up, the name of Christ's Church is the One, Holy, Catholic and Roman Church. This Church alone possesses the authority to teach men what they must do and believe to be saved. Since all other sects do not have any of the marks of the True Church, they have absolutely no authority to teach in Christ's name.

XIX

The Church is a Moral Miracle

THE USE OF THE four marks will always remain the best way to prove the divine origin of Christ's Church for this was the means given by Christ Himself. Facility in finding the True Church is important, for, since the Church is to be the guide to salvation for all men, its finding must be within the reach of every investigator and not only within that of the learned.

The proof for the divine origin of the Church from the possession of the four marks needs no corroboration. It is complete and valid as it stands. But a better appreciation and realization of the significance of the Roman Catholic Church's divinity can be gained by examining the unshaken stability which it has exhibited for the past two thousand years.

The stability of the Church as an argument for its divinity is not new. It was foreshadowed within a few weeks after Christ's ascension into heaven. On that occasion the leaders of the Jews strictly forbade the Apostles to preach in His Name. When repeated threats and imprisonments did not deter the disciples, these same leaders threatened them with death. But during one of the sessions, Gamaliel, a Pharisee, stood up and reminded the Sanhedrin of how a certain Theodas and Judas the Galilean, being merely human, had failed in their ventures. Then concerning the Apostles he said, "Keep away from these men—for if this plan or work is of men, it will be overthrown; but if it is of God, you will not be able to overthrow it." (Acts 5:38)

We cannot but admire the perfectly straightforward manner in which Gamaliel appraised the problem before the Sanhedrin.

Christian writers have often pointed to the stability of the Church as proof of its divinity. Origen noticed and urged it as early as the middle of the Third Century.[1] And in the Fifth Century when many were looking for miracles and unusual signs from God to bolster perhaps a faltering faith, St. Augustine told them that they need but to behold the unshaken stability of the Church. He said that the Church was an ever present argument against those who rejected the historical value of the Gospels or who were too unlettered to grasp the meaning of the marks of the Church.

The proof for the divinity of the Catholic Church from its stability especially appeals to students of history. Its full force is felt when one compares the endurance of admittedly human organizations in history with that of the Church. The more comparisons are made, the more real does the argument become.

When we study the histories of the different nations which have appeared on earth, we notice a certain pattern in their rise and fall. The causes of their appearance and disintegration are almost stereotyped. The purpose of this chapter is to sketch briefly how the factors which have accounted for the rise and fall of man-made agencies have not affected the Church, thereby proving that they are two essentially different types of organizations.

1. *Factors of Rise*—The student of history will observe that many empires and societies were founded by men who shrewdly took advantage of weakness at home or abroad to seize power and then to extend it until they had carved out vast empires. The domains of Alexander the Great, Caesar and Napoleon

1. *Contra Celsum* Bk. II, Ch. 79.

belong to this category. They were established and maintained by armed might. The Roman Empire ranks well in history as a firm and stable government. But it grew by military conquest. Supremacy was safeguarded by such precautions as a fine system of roads that radiated from the city of Rome to the far-flung parts of the empire-roads over which troops could be swiftly transported to crush rebellion. Many provinces were governed by men of military experience who could meet any threat to the security of the state with force. What has been said of the Roman Empire could be said of many other political organizations.

Many non-religious factors played an important part in the start and growth of the principal religious groups which have survived to the present time. Notice these factors. Mohammedanism was propagated by the sword. When the Anglican Church was founded by royal decree, all other religious sects were put on the proscribed list. In the Teutonic countries, Lutheranism would not have made the strides that it did if it had not received an impetus from the dissatisfaction over unworthy prelates, from the appeal to the nationalism of especially the Germans, and from the hope of the princes of acquiring confiscated Church property. The Orthodox Church would not have made the progress it did if the ethnic opposition between East and West had been left out of consideration.

In spite of the fact that the secular empires were built up and maintained by armed might, they have perished from the face of the earth and are of scarcely more than historical interest today. It would indeed be a serious mistake to think that the Protestant sects have survived the centuries in the condition in which they were founded. They have and are still going through a process of division and disintegration. The Lutheran Church is not one Church. There are some 22 different autonomous Lutheran sects each professing belief in a different set of doctrines. Anglicanism is broken up into the

High, Low and Broad Churches; there are 14 nationally autonomous Orthodox Churches; 15 different Presbyterian sects, 17 Methodist sects, 15 Baptist sects and some 12 different Mennonite sects. From this we can conclude that survival of name is no proof of stability.

We now ask whether or not the rise of the Roman Catholic Church had anything in common with the rise of secular empires or the rise of the religious sects of the Sixteenth Century. Notice how according to human standards this church should not have survived. Its founder was Jesus Christ who did not have the wealth, power and influence of a Caesar or Napoleon. A—He was born of a race of people who were despised in ancient times. The Emperor Claudius expelled the Jews from Rome in 42 A.D. and in some places they lived in the continual fear of being attacked by the populace.[2] B—He was associated with a Jewish province whose people were hated by other Jews. "Can anything good come from Galilee?"[3] they said. Of His twelve Apostles, all were Galileans except one—Judas Iscariot, the Judean. C—His enemies made every effort to obliterate his memory. To attempt to do this, they put Him to death in the most shameful way that pagan barbarism could devise—crucifixion. The Jews attempted to discredit the reports of His resurrection[4] and took measures to prevent His followers from preaching in His name.[5] D—He chose to be represented first by twelve men who were neither educated nor influential and who plied such shunned occupations as that of fisherman or of publican. Of these twelve, one betrayed Him, one denied Him and all but one deserted Him when He was crucified. E—He sent the Apostles to teach doctrines

2. Papyrus fragments found in Egypt show that the Jews of ancient times were often the object of race riots. Cf. Loeb Classical Library, *Select Papyri,* Vol. II, Nos. 212 and 298, translated by Hunt and Edgar (London; Heinemann, 1934).

3. John 7:40.

4. Matt. 28:11.

5. Acts 5:28.

which in the natural sense were not attractive. The people were asked to believe truths which were difficult and even impossible to understand and repugnant to minds given over to intellectual pride. Christ's unbending code of morals made no concessions to nations steeped in sensuality. As a climax, the Apostles were sent to preach to strangers and to instill a faith that would withstand the rigors of persecution and death. F— Far from catering to nationalism and national pride, He said that His religion would know no distinction between Jew and Gentile, Greek and Barbarian.

Instead of using the devices that the founders of secular empires used, Christ seems to have consciously avoided them so that His Church might more easily be recognized as a divine organization. In the face of the obstacles which we have enumerated, a human agency would not have made notable progress. But how did Christ's Church progress? The anti-Christian critic Ernest Renan said that in the first Century Christianity was like a flash of lightning which almost simultaneously lighted up the three peninsulas of Asia Minor, Greece and Italy. The rationalist Harnack summed up the early progress of the Church in these terms:

The impression which the Church Fathers of the Fourth Century had that their faith had spread with incomprehensible rapidity was well founded. Seventy years after the establishment of the first congregation of Jewish converts at Antioch, Pliny writes in the strongest terms of the expansion of Christianity in far distant Pontus and regards the other cults in that province as imperilled. Seventy years later the controversy regarding the celebration of Easter shows the existence of a Christian ecclesiastical confederation reaching from Lyons to Edessa. After another seventy years the Emperor Decius declares that he would rather tolerate a rival emperor in Rome than a Christian bishop and in less than seventy more years the cross is affixed to Roman field standards.[6]

6. Brunsmann-Preuss, *Fundamental Theology* (St. Louis; B. Herder Book Co., 1929), II, 498.

The conclusion to this first observation is that the rise of the Roman Catholic Church had nothing in common with the rise of the human organizations of history. Christ resorted to none of the practices of humankind in establishing His Church. But the significant point is that while the great empires of history have perished and the religious sects have disintegrated, the Catholic Church has survived and has remained intact.

2. *Internal Conditions*—History shows that well planned beginnings are no guarantee that nations and societies will long endure. After their establishment, internal conditions have often brought about their doom. Two frequent causes of collapse have been inefficient administration on the part of key rulers and insurgent nationalism.

In general, highly centralized governments have been the least stable. For one person to control and coordinate effectively the many departments of a government considerable ability is required and for such a government to endure demands a succession of able rulers. But efficient and conscientious rulers have not always succeeded to power in many highly centralized governments and so those nations have eventually disappeared.

The Roman Catholic Church has a very highly centralized government for we have seen that her supreme rulers possess a primacy of jurisdiction over the entire church. The legislation that the Sovereign Pontiff enacts does not need the approval of anyone else in the Church to be binding. He does not have to give an account of the manner in which he rules the Church to anyone except God and his own conscience. He is the supreme teacher of the Church on earth. With such a concentration of power in the hands of this one person, one is tempted to think that stability and continuance in existence of the Church depends on his ability to rule. If he is efficient, then the church will prosper and be vigorous. If he is weak and inefficient, then it will stagger for a while and then collapse. History shows that this has been only too true in the case of secular governments and human organizations.

Does the Catholic Church owe her stability to the efficiency of her supreme rulers? In the first centuries when one would think that the infant Church most needed the guidance of her chief shepherds, we notice that with few exceptions, the first forty of them were martyred or exiled. The Emperor Valerian thought that the dictum "Strike the shepherd and the flock will be dispersed" could effectively be applied to the Church for his persecution differs from the other nine in that it was aimed primarily against the leaders of the Church.

It is not difficult to prove that all of the popes were not the able administrators that this type of government demands. Nor is it difficult to show that in some countries, especially in times when the Church was wealthy, she was ruled by unworthy prelates. These particular prelates were persons who abused their power and were not sources of edification to the people. Some of them shamelessly bought and sold benefices and in their role of temporal ruler insisted on the right to heavily tax their subjects but did not fulfill the corresponding duties of their office. Some of them seemed unaware of their duties to God and to their flock.

Critics have seized upon the point of the scandals in the Church with vigor. Luther went so far as to say that these abuses so destroyed the power of the Church for doing good that nothing of it could be salvaged and that another Church should replace it. Little did Luther and other critics realize that the more real or imaginary abuses of Renaissance times they bring to light, the more attention they call to the Great Western Schism of the Middle Ages, the more they are strengthening the arguments for the divinity of the Church. If the Catholic Church was not a divine institution it could never have survived the inefficiency of some of her rulers.

A second internal situation which has wrecked the unity not only of political but also of religious organizations has been insurgent nationalism. The people of one race are usually very reluctant to be governed by a ruler of another no matter how benevolent he might be. And their reluctance has often resulted in a rebellion which paved the way for the dissolution of the realm. Some powers transplanted ethnic groups to keep them weak. In Roman times Celts were transplanted to Asia Minor, Egyptians to the Balkans and Greeks to Gaul. The empires of Napoleon and Francis Joseph might have longer endured if they had not been made up of so many different nationalities. Nationalism has prevented the Orthodox Church of eastern Europe from being unified in government. These Churches are still broken up into fourteen nationally autonomous groups. Several of the leaders of the Protestant Revolt realized that their sect would have a better chance of survival if it was organized along national and racial lines. This was the case with the Church of England, the Dutch and Hungarian Reformed Churches, the national churches in the Scandinavian countries and many others.

If the Roman Catholic Church was but a human organization, insurgent nationalism would have wrecked it centuries ago. But it never found language or race a barrier to its spread. In ancient times, it spread simultaneously among the Latins and Greeks, Semites and Slavs, Celts and Goths. In modern times, it has outstripped explorers and merchants in finding its way among the natives of the New World and the Orient.

As the Church spread among these races, it did not break up into autonomous groups. It spread as a perfect unity. All of its members look upon the Roman Pontiff not merely as a symbol of unity as the British Monarch is looked upon but as a person possessing a primacy of jurisdiction. The Roman Catholic Church is sustained by the power of God for no human society could be spread among so many races of people for such a period of time as it has and yet remain unshaken in stability and unity.

3. *External Forces*—Every century of the history of the world has seen its share of wars of conquest. That some of

these wars have been successful is evidenced by the ever changing political map of the world. Foreign invasion has played a major role in the destruction of practically every great empire in history. The list of nations which fall into this category is too long for us to enumerate here.

What foreign invasion is in the political sphere, persecution is in the religious sphere. It is simply attack from without. Just as invasions were designed to destroy or weaken a political entity, so persecutions were designed to destroy or weaken the Church. Many persecutions against the Church were as carefully planned[7] and as systematically carried out as any military campaign. Civil powers survived external invasion only when they could match the armed might of their aggressor. The Catholic Church has survived external attack such as has never been levelled against any civil or religious group even though it never recruited armies to repel them. There has been scarcely a century in which some major persecutions were not directed against it. Yet the fact that it has survived proves that it is not a merely human society but a Church sustained by the hand of God.

Do you not see how they are thrown before the wild beasts to make them disown the Lord, and they refuse to be overcome? Do you not see that the more of them are penalized, the more their numbers grow. Such things do not point to a human agency. Here is the power of God, here the proofs of His abiding presence.[8]

Persecutions have produced martyrs. It is impossible to explain by natural means the constancy which the martyrs of the Church have exhibited. There were martyrs of both sexes, of every age level and from all walks of life. But amidst the great diversity in age and in tortures, there was a common note which bound all of them together. They all suffered and died

7. Tertullian, *Scorpiace* 10.
8. *Letter to Diognetus* Ch. 7, trans. by James A. Kleist, S.J., in "Ancient Christian Writers" series (Westminster; Newman, 1948). This is probably a 2nd Century writing.

out of loyalty to Christ and to attest the divinity of Christianity. "We do not see in them soldiers who sacrifice their all in defending their fatherland, nor conquerors who set out to violently subdue an unexplored land; nor the daring who throw themselves into fire or water to save another who is in danger of death; nor the philanthropic who give their lives for humanity; nor revolutionaries; nor the discontent who rebel against a tyrant in the hope of deposing him; nor the fanatic; nor the superstitious who act on impulse."[9] To the victims of the persecutions, martyrdom was a profession of faith.

The best known of all the persecutions were those decreed against the Church by the Roman Emperors. Words cannot describe the afflictions to which the martyrs were subjected. Tertullian repeatedly proved that the only reason why the Christians were persecuted was because of their religion. He systematically destroyed the other excuses by which the civil authorities tried to justify their stern action.

In Roman times when a Christian was captured and accused of violating the civil law by being a Christian, he was put on trial and given the choice of either giving up his religion or of being tortured. If he refused to give up his religion he was subjected either to moral or to physical torture or both.[10] We read in authentic narrative that some of the moral tortures which the early Christians underwent were to have all their property confiscated, to be stripped of rank and civil office, to be deprived of the right to appeal the case in court, to be exiled from family, for women to be forced into brothels.

Roman law forbade the affliction of unusual or cruel torments, but in the case of the Christian martyrs these laws were simply disregarded. Christians were put to death in many ways. They were beheaded, devoured by wild beasts, burned at stake,

9. Gallina, *I Martiri Dei Primi Secoli* (Firenze; Salani, 1942), p. 13.
10. The transcripts of many of these trials are extant today together with the details of the executions of the martyrs. Two famous accounts are the well authenticated *Martyrium of St. Polycarp* and the *Passio of SS Felicitas and Perpetua.*

stoned to death, thrown into quick-lime, roasted on the grid-iron, stabbed to death, gored by wild bulls, suffocated, sewed up in a sack with poisonous reptiles, strangled, entombed alive, put on the rack, torn with hooks, shot with arrows, rolled up in pitch and burned, frozen to death and hanged. Of all the ways that pagan barbarism invented to put a person to death, none was considered more disgraceful and more ig-nominious than crucifixion. It was usually reserved for slaves but many Christian nobles and freedmen suffered in this way. No coup de grâce was permitted in this type of execution and so sometimes death was very slow in coming. We speak here of the Roman martyrs. The martyrs of other ages and other lands suffered as dreadfully and as courageously as did those of ancient times.

Attacks as fierce and persistent as those levelled against the Church in the form of persecutions would have weakened and destroyed human organizations. But strange to say, they have served to revitalize the Church. She has flourished in the midst of adversity so that Tertullian could rightly say, "The blood of the martyrs is the seed of the Church." The most glorious period in the history of the Church was not the time of the Renaissance when she was wealthy and respected; it was rather, the ante-Nicene age when she shuddered under the impact of ten general persecutions.

The conclusions gathered from the several observations which have been made is that the Roman Catholic Church is not the product of human efforts, for it has not been overcome by the same forces which have affected man-made organiza-tions. The Church is essentially different from them. It is like the house of which Christ speaks in the Gospel when He said, "And the rain fell and the floods came, and they beat upon that house, and it fell not, for it was founded on a rock." (Matt. 7:25). Its unshaken stability can only be explained by saying that it is sustained by divine power and is therefore a work of God.

XX

The Infallibility of the Church

ONCE IT HAS BEEN established that the One, Holy, Catholic and Roman Church is the agency founded by Christ to teach all men what they must do and believe to be saved, it is easy to show that she is an infallible teacher. *Infallibility as it is used in this chapter is defined as a supernatural or God-given endowment by which the Roman Catholic Church enjoys divine assistance in unerringly defining and teaching a divine doctrine.* The Church must have this endowment to carry out her teaching office.

The proof for the infallibility of the Church is developed in this way. Christ proved that He is God and so is infinitely truthful. He taught what all men must do and believe to be saved. His doctrines are valid for all ages but Christ did not choose to remain on earth for all time to teach them. He confided this task to a teaching agency called the Roman Catholic Church. Now it is clearly against the divine wisdom of Christ to be represented on earth by a Church which would or even could teach false doctrines. Christ authorized the Church to teach with exactly the same authority which He had while on earth, as can be gathered from these texts:

"He who hears you, hears me; and he who rejects you, rejects me; and he who rejects me, rejects him who sent me." [Luke 10:16]

And he said to them, "Go into the whole world and preach the gospel to every creature. He who believes and is baptized shall be saved, but he who does not believe shall be condemned." [Mark 16:15]

It is absurd to think that God would authorize a Church to teach even some false doctrines and then make a person's salvation depend on the acceptance of these false doctrines, for He said that whoever did not receive His doctrines as the Church taught them would be condemned.

The note of infallibility will be an endowment of the Church as long as there is need on earth for the Church. Since this need will exist until the end of time, it follows that the Church will always be infallible. Indeed, when Christ commissioned His Church to teach, He promised to remain with it until the consummation of the world.[1]

The question which naturally arises here is, "In whom, today, does this divinely-promised infallibility reside?" It resides in the successors of those whom Christ authorized to teach in His name. Christ personally entrusted the task of teaching to St. Peter[2] and the Apostles. The successor of St. Peter is the bishop of Rome or the Pope; the successors of the Apostles are the bishops of the Church. These are the official teachers of the Church and under several well defined conditions God protects them from making an error in teaching.

In certain circumstances the pope himself can make infallible pronouncements. By this we mean that the statement of the pope does not need the approval of any group in order to be free from error. He is not subject to anyone in the exercise of his teaching office. He can make an infallible pronouncement whenever he feels the need for it. This can be gathered from the fact that he is the successor of St. Peter in the primacy. In the Church he is the foundation rock, the keeper of the keys, and the shepherd of the flock of Christ. He has the fullness of power in the Church. But he would not have this

1. Matt. 28:18-20.
2. Matt. 16:16-19; Luke 22:32; John 21:15-17.

fullness of power if he himself did not have the power to speak infallibly. It will not do to split the primacy of jurisdiction of the pope into the power to teach and the power to rule, and then to grant that he has the supreme power to rule but deny that he has the supreme power to teach. To admit that the pope has supreme power implies that he has the power to teach as well as to rule.

The pope is an infallible teacher when these three conditions are verified:

1. He must not be speaking as a private theologian or in the capacity of the bishop of the diocese of Rome or even as the patriarch of the West. He must be speaking *ex cathedra,* that is, as the supreme teacher of the universal Church.

2. He must not be merely advancing an opinion or making an exhortation but must be defining or definitely settling an article of faith or morals or a matter intimately connected with it.

3. He must clearly intend that the doctrine which he defines be accepted by all the members of the universal Church.

When these three conditions are present, God protects the pope from committing an error.

Infallibility in teaching does not reside exclusively in the pope. It will be remembered that Christ also designated the Apostles as His official teachers and so they, too, were inerrant. The bishops of the Church are infallible because they are the successors of the Apostles. But each bishop by himself does not have the endowment of inerrancy. Inerrancy is a prerogative of the bishops taken as a group and not individually for when Christ commissioned the Apostles to teach, He commissioned them as a group.[3] This can be proved from several passages in the Gospels. Under certain conditions, they too are

3. Matt. 28:18–20; Mark 3:13–19; Mark 16:15; John 15:16; John 17:18–20; John 20:21.

infallible either when gathered in general council or when dispersed throughout the world.

Although the doctrine of infallibility was formally defined in 1870 by the Vatican Council, it was taught long before then. We have seen that the Church's endowment to teach without error is clearly contained in the Gospels. This inerrancy was also held in ancient times as can be established from extant literature of that period. Every text that can be cited to prove the primacy of the Roman Pontiff is implicitly a testimony in favor of his infallible teaching authority. And these texts can be quoted from writings composed as early as the First Century. But the oldest writing which explicitly refers to the supreme teaching authority of the pope is the *Adversus Haereses* of St. Irenaeus composed in the Second Century.

In a remarkable passage,[4] St. Irenaeus reminds the faithful of the principle which must guide them in distinguishing truth from the Gnostic error rampant at the time. He says that they must hold firmly to the rule of faith. That rule is not something buried in the historical past. It was the voice of those who could be proven to be the successors of the Apostles. Their teaching is the touchstone of truth in religion. The writer was quick to observe that this was a tremendous task for the ordinary person to consult all of these teachers individually, and besides this was unnecessary. He could arrive at the same truth by learning the teaching of the Church of Rome. All Christian communities had to conform their teaching with that of the Roman Pontiff because of the latter's preeminent authority. The author then writes that celebrated passage in which he enumerates the twelve pontiffs who ruled the Roman See from Peter to Eleutherius then presiding.

The testimony of St. Irenaeus was repeated by many writers in later times and St. Augustine did but summarize[5] it when

4. *Adv. Haer.* Bk. III. iii. 1.
5. *Contra Iulianum* Bk. I. 13.

he wrote that after the Roman Pontiff has defined a doctrine there is no more room for controversy.

From what has been said in the above paragraphs, we notice that the source of the pope's or bishops' infallibility is not their own native prudence or learning. It is the divine wisdom of the Holy Ghost. Nor does infallibility mean that the one who possesses it cannot commit sin as many misinformed people think it means. This prerogative was not given to the pope or to the bishops for their own personal benefit, but as an assurance to the people of the world that the Church is the custodian and unerring interpreter of divinely revealed truth.

The Church is infallible when her pronouncements are on points which concern these three topics:

1. When she teaches that a certain doctrine is explicitly or implicitly contained in the deposit of revelation made to man by God.

2. When she speaks on a subject which is necessary to explain or defend the deposit of faith.

3. When she speaks on a subject which is necessary or very useful to obtain the goal of revelation which is the sanctification and salvation of men.

Having proved the infallible authority of the Church, the student is in a position to note where she says the doctrines of revelation are to be found. She has defined that the fonts or sources of revelation are Sacred Scripture and Sacred Tradition, the Written and Unwritten Word of God. These are the infallible decrees of the Church on this matter:

The Holy, Ecumenical, General Synod of Trent . . . following the example of the orthodox Fathers, receives and venerates with equal devotion and reverence all the books of both the Old and the New Testaments, since the one God is the author of both, as also the aforesaid traditions, whether pertaining to faith or to morals, as delivered by the very mouth of Christ or dictated by the Holy Spirit, and preserved in the Catholic Church by the unfailing tradition. And lest any doubt should arise as to which are the books received by this Synod, it has seemed good to append to this decree a list of them.

The following, then, are the books of the Old Testament:

The five books of Moses, namely, Genesis, Exodus, Leviticus, Numbers, Deuteronomy; then, Josue, Judges, Ruth; the four books of Kings, the two books of Paralipomena; the two of Esdras, the first namely, and the second which is called Nehemias; Tobias, Judith, Esther, Job; the Davidic psalter of 150 Psalms; Parables (Proverbs), Ecclesiastes, Canticle of Canticles, Wisdom, Ecclesiasticus; Isaias, Jeremias, Baruch, Ezechiel, Daniel; the twelve minor prophets, namely Osee, Joel, Amos, Abdias, Jonas, Micheas, Nahum, Habacuc, Sophonias, Aggeus, Zacharias, Malachias; the two books of Machabees, namely the first and the second.

The following are the books of the New Testament,

Four Gospels, namely the ones according to Matthew, Mark, Luke and John; the Acts of the Apostles written by Luke the Evangelist; the fourteen epistles of Paul the Apostle, namely one to the Romans, two to the Corinthians, one to the Galatians, one to the Ephesians, one to the Philippians, one to the Colossians, two to the Thessalonians, two to Timothy, one to Titus, one to Philemon, and one to the Hebrews; two epistles of Peter the Apostle; three epistles of John the Apostle; one epistle of James; one epistle of Jude; and the Apocalypse of John the Apostle.

If anyone shall not receive these entire books with all their parts as they have been wont to be read in the Catholic Church and as they are contained in the old Latin edition, and whosoever shall knowingly and of set purpose contemn the aforesaid traditions, let him be anathema.[6]

6. H. Pope, *The Catholic Student's "Aids" to the Bible* (London; Burns, Oates & Washbourne, 1926), I, 152.

Decree of the Council of Trent approved by Pope Paul III in 1546 and appearing in Denzinger Enchiridion Symbolorum 783:

Furthermore one must believe with divine and Catholic faith, all those doctrines which are contained either in the written word of God or in tradition, and proposed by the Church whether in a solemn or ordinary pronouncement and by the universal teaching body, to be believed as divine revelation.

Decree of the Council of the Vatican approved by Pope Pius IX in 1870 and appearing in Denzinger 1792.

As can be seen from the above definitions, the sources of revelation are Sacred Scripture and Sacred Tradition, the Written and the Unwritten Word of God. They are the reservoirs into which God has poured His revelation to man. Since the Roman Catholic Church is the agency which was authorized by Christ to teach men what they must do and believe to be saved, it follows that it was to her alone that Christ confided these fonts of revelation. For spurious teaching agencies or churches to take over the books of Sacred Scripture and interpret them privately is clearly an instance of unauthorized usurpation. They have no authorization to use the Scriptures as they please. And this denial of the use of the Scriptures for misuse to false churches is as old as Christianity itself. Tertullian urged the same argument in the closing years of the Second Century when he denied the use of the Gospels to heretics who would distort them. At that time he forcefully wrote:

Since this is the case, in order that the truth may be adjudged to belong to us, "as many as walk according to the rule," which the Church has handed down from the Apostles, the Apostles from Christ and Christ from God, the reason of our position is clear, when it determines that heretics ought not to be allowed to challenge an appeal to the Scriptures, since we, without the Scriptures, prove that they have nothing to do with the Scriptures. For as they are heretics they cannot be true Christians because it is not from Christ that which they pursue of their own mere choice, and from the pursuit incur and admit the name of heretics. Thus, not being Christians they have no right to appeal to the Christian Scriptures; and it may very fairly be said to them, "Who are you? When and whence did you come? As you are none of mine, what did you do with that which is mine? Indeed, Marcion, by what right do you hue my wood? By whose permission, Valentinus, are you diverting the streams of my fountain? By what power, Apelles, are you removing my landmarks? This is my property. Why are you, the rest, sowing and feeding here at your pleasure? This is my property. I have long possessed it; I possessed it before you. I hold sure title deeds from the original owners, themselves, to whom the estate belonged. I am the heir of the Apostles."[7]

It is regrettable that the result of the unwarranted appropriation of Scripture and Tradition on the part of spurious teaching agencies has been to confuse men concerning those things which pertain to salvation. Many times they have been torn from their spiritual moorings and left to drift and founder amidst the storms of uncertainty and false doctrine. Would that all men would cease their wanderings and seek shelter within the fold of Holy Mother the Church, for

Ubi Petrus, ibi Ecclesia;
Ubi Ecclesia, ibi vita aeterna.[8]

7. *De Praescriptione Haereticorum* Ch. 37. Cf. also Ch. 15 and 19.

8. Trans., "Where Peter is, there is the Church; Where the Church is, there is eternal life." This saying is from a sermon of St. Ambrose. It appears on the wall of the cupola of the Cathedral of Milan.

XXI

Act of Faith

ONCE THE AUTHORITY of the Roman Catholic Church has been established, it follows that to believe the doctrines she teaches is logical and necessary for they are God's. Apologetics can only demonstrate that the obligation to believe is sound and cogent. But it cannot force one to believe against his will; it cannot compel acceptance of the doctrines God has revealed. St. Augustine said, "A man may enter the Church unwillingly; he may approach the altar unwillingly, he may receive the Sacrament unwillingly, but he cannot believe unless he wills it." It is, therefore, one thing to present a valid proof and quite another matter to get people to accept it. The fact that some refuse to accept a proof does not mean that it is not a sound one. Prejudice and irrational motivation can distort correct thinking.

1. IMPORTANCE OF FAITH—

Concerning the act of faith, the Council of Trent teaches that it is the beginning and root of all justification.[1] "For all who have come to the use of reason, actual theological faith is necessary for salvation for unless we are moved by a true act of faith to believe in God, we cannot move toward Him as towards our supernatural goal."[2]

Since our goal in life is supernatural, natural reason alone

1. D–801.
2. Henry Davis, S.J., *Moral and Pastoral Theology*, 4th Edition (London; Sheed and Ward, 1945), I, 275.

is not sufficient to dispose us to it. Faith is the beginning and foundation of all justification. There is no substitute for it.

An act of faith in the doctrines proposed to us by the Church is defined as: *a firm assent of the intellect to a truth revealed by God made by command of the will assisted by divine grace and motivated by the authority of God, Who cannot deceive or be deceived.*

A. *Firm assent of intellect*—The intellect is man's knowing power. Its object is to grasp truth. Apologetics proves that there can be no reasonable doubt that God transmits truth to man through the medium known as His Church. Since He can never err, our acceptance of His truths must be firm and unwavering.

B. *Under command of will*—Even though the evidence for the authority of the Church is conclusive, there is nothing about it which prevents a person from deliberately blinding himself to its cogency. Such a one does not want to believe. He has some irrational motive in turning away from the evidence. An act of faith shows that the inquirer freely chooses to accept valid evidence presented to him.

C. *Assisted by divine grace*—Man is born in the natural state. Of himself he cannot do anything which is above his powers. With his natural powers he clearly cannot perform a supernatural act which is precisely what an act of faith is. For this he must receive supernatural help. That help is divine grace.

D. *Motivated by the authority of God Who cannot deceive* —Since God is perfect in every respect it follows that it is absolutely impossible for Him to deceive for this would be against the attribute of His infinite Truthfulness. This is the strongest of all motives for believing.

2. TRUTHS TO BE BELIEVED—

All the truths that God has revealed must be believed for His authority vouches for the truthfulness of each and everyone of them. To deny even one of them would be to deny the authority of God in revealing. But it is not necessary that everyone should know all of these truths explicitly or in set terms for this is a difficult task for even a person with an above average intelligence. Everyone, however, must accept the entire content of divine revelation implicitly for the motive of the act of faith extends to the entire set of doctrines.

There are certain doctrines that must be known explicitly, that is, in set terms. A person must know precisely what they are and must be able to name them. It is not enough that one accepts these articles when he accepts others. In view of Christ's command to His Church that it teach all men, there is a supplementary command that all men believe what the Church teaches. According to the Church, the doctrines pertaining to the four categories are the minimum which all not in danger of death must believe by necessity of precept.[2]

a. *Faith*—He must know the articles summarized in the Apostles' Creed. b. *Morals*—He must know the substance of the Commandments of God and of the Church. c. *Prayer*—He must know the Lord's Prayer. d. *Practice*—He must know the meaning of the sacraments of Baptism, Penance, Holy Eucharist and the others at the time of their reception. It is well to remember that unless these articles are learned and memorized in a formula they will easily be forgotten. The precept to know these articles is grave, for without them it is impossible to lead a Christian life.

Dangers to Faith

Having shown the strong motives, sound logic and divine grace which stands behind our faith, it would seem that once one possessed it, it would be difficult to lose it. But this unfortunately is not the case. We shall see that the gift of faith can be abused, weakened and even lost. All sins are, of course,

2. Noldin, S.J., *Theologia Moralis,* 27th ed. (Innsbruck, 1941), II, 13–14.

to be avoided but the sin of loss of faith is especially to be avoided for faith is the foundation of the supernatural life of the soul. St. Paul writes,

It is impossible for those who were once enlightened [Baptism], who have both tasted the heavenly gift [Holy Eucharist], and become partakers of the Holy Spirit [Confirmation], who have moreover tasted the good word of God [instruction], and the powers of the world to come, and then have fallen away, to be renewed again to repentance. [Hebrews 6:4]

This passage from the writings of the Apostle to the Gentiles has been verified only too often in real life. Loss of faith is usually preceded by a period in which factors which weaken the faith are allowed to operate unchecked. Attention is here called to the principal ones.

1. *Ignorance*—A person cannot want what he does not know. If a person does not exert himself to learn the doctrines of faith or, once having learned them, permits himself to forget them, it follows that they will not be a very great force in his life. This state of affairs is but a prelude to the complete extinction of the light of faith. The enemies of the Church have realized that they could deliver a damaging blow to her effectiveness if they could keep the people ignorant of the doctrines she teaches. Ignorance has been a major factor why some "Catholic" countries are only nominally Catholic.

In seeing to it that children receive proper religious instruction there is no substitute for the Catholic school. It is only there that religion is put on a par with profane studies and receives the attention it should receive. The danger to the faith of children attending non-Catholic elementary schools is a *negative* one. By this we mean that the danger is caused by their being deprived of what they should receive. When children see that religion is not taught them, they soon draw the conclusion that it must not be very important. Their psy-

chological reaction is indeed detrimental. And it is this conclusion that parents—especially those in a mixed marriage—
underscore when they neglect or refuse to send their children
to Catholic schools. Every pastor will readily admit that week-
ly catechism classes are not the best solution to the problem
of dispelling ignorance of the doctrines of faith in the minds
of children.

The danger to the faith of Catholic students attending non-
Catholic colleges is positive. The danger is double. The students do not only suffer by being deprived of the instruction
they should receive but they are often forced to take courses
which are frankly pernicious to the faith.

It is certainly no secret that many courses which for public
consumption are labelled "objective" and "non-sectarian" are
anything but that. Many branches in such fields as comparative religion, science, philosophy, history, sociology, psychol-
ogy, ethics and others are often studied from text-books with
an anti-Catholic coloring or which receive this coloring when
they pass through the hands of certain professors. It is the exceptional college where the majority of the Catholic students
take part in the Newman Club program, and even those who
do, do not receive the training in religion that they would in
a Catholic college. Secular education is indeed one of the more
notable causes of defection from the faith.

2. *Pride*—A second cause of loss of faith is intellectual pride.
This pride attaches an exaggerated importance to unaided reason in the discovery of truth. It holds that all propositions
must pass the test of comprehensibility before they should be
accepted. When a person in this frame of mind examines the
mysteries which God has revealed, he immediately rejects
them because he cannot fully understand their intrinsic nature.

The possession of a fine intellect is no guarantee that it
will not be abused. Every century has seen men of superior
intelligence succumb to the stirring of intellectual pride. The

Church has seen how these heretics could be impressive to the unsuspecting and unwary. She has seen how persuasively they could clothe their error in the spoken or written word. To protect her children against those bent on deception, the Church has exposed these propagators of falsehood. She has excommunicated those holding the error and placed their books containing it on the Index.

The truly great intellects of the Church like St. Thomas Aquinas and St. Augustine realized the mind's limitations in discovering truth. They saw how small were the gleanings of unaided reason when compared to truths made known to us by revelation. To them, to be taught by God through the Church was a tremendous privilege. Instead of being shackled as rationalists think, the mind possessed truth which it could not otherwise attain. This made them at once humble and grateful.

3. *Sensuality*—A last cause of loss of faith is sensuality and especially sins of impurity. A lively faith makes one concentrate on the spiritual and heavenly. Sensuality blunts the spiritual sense and inflates the importance of earthly pleasures. If one has faith and a keen sense of right and wrong, then to him sins of sensuality will be disquieting, will produce remorse. He soon wishes to ease his tortured state of mind. He sees that he cannot have them both. They are almost mutually exclusive. He must make a choice. He chooses sensuality. Faith immediately begins to lose the place it once had in his life. It is being crowded out. If this aversion from the light is prolonged, then complete loss of faith is near. It is the opinion of important spiritual writers that sensuality is the most dangerous of all the causes that can attack one's faith.

Epilogue

I was an eye to the blind, a leg to the lame and a Father to the poor. (Wisdom)

THE PEOPLE of the pagan nations of pre-Christian times excite our pity as we see them stumbling from pleasure to pleasure and from error to error in the hope of finding truth and happiness. They "looked and looked but could not see; they listened and listened but could not hear." They packed the fora of Rome and Athens and Antioch and Ephesus to listen to every itinerant teacher who promised them a solution to the riddle of life. They were a ready audience for everyone who said he could give them an answer to the burning questions, "What are we here for and where are we going?" But the pagans soon tired of the despair-producing sophistry of the Epicureans and the hardened, inhuman apathy of the Stoics. They were quick to perceive the empty ritual of the Mithric cults and the shallow worship of the Egyptian deities. In brief, they weighed in the balance the best that paganism could offer and found it wanting. And when they saw that they could not rid themselves of their blindness, they sat by the roadside of life and like Bar-Timaeus began to cry out, "O God, that we may see."

It eventually came to pass that those nations which sat "in darkness and in the shadow of death" saw a great light—a light that the darkness would never comprehend. That light was Christ in the Church. Nineteen centuries have passed since the days when Christ walked the streets of Jerusalem and the roads of Galilee. Several civilizations have come and gone,

many generations of men have appeared and faded, customs
and governments have changed, the heroic exploits of the
world's great have become enshrouded in the mist of years.
But human nature has not changed. Man's hopes and fears,
his aspirations and disappointments are the same. Today as in
ancient times, his thirst for truth is not quenched at the foun-
tains of material science, or pointless speculation or meaningless theory. Today as in former days, man needs the shelter
of the teaching authority of Holy Mother the Church.

The Church has never forgotten the important role she has
in the lives of men. She has been keenly conscious that the
greatest enemy of Christ is ignorance of Christ and for this
reason, of all the educational crusades which have been conducted on earth, none has been so relentless as hers. She has
made her influence felt at all times and in the most diverse
places. Read and marvel at her perseverance. The Church was
present when the White Fathers built thatch-roofed schools
in Africa and the Franciscans built mission schools in Cali-
fornia; her Maryknoll Fathers were the harbingers of the "rising sun" in the Far East and the Oblate Fathers were the
"northern lights" to the Eskimos. She reminded the materialistic philosophers of the Nineteenth and Twentieth Centuries
that "not by bread alone does man live." She translated the
catechism in the languages of the Hurons and Iroquois with
an Isaac Jogues and Charles Garnier; she already possessed the
waters of eternal life when she accompanied the Spanish explorers searching for the fountain of youth; she waited on the
wharves of Cartagena with a Peter Claver to dispense to the
incoming slaves the truth that would make men free; she
listened as the natives of the Orient greeted a Francis Xavier
with the faint chant of "Blessed is he who comes in the name
of the Lord." Her doctrines breathed lasting life into the mar-
ble worked by the hand of a Michaelangelo and the bronze
shaped by the hand of a Donatello. The sharp scimitar of the
crescented flag was no match for the pen wielded by her hum-

ble friar from Aquino. She proudly laid the cornerstones of her great universities at Oxford, Cambridge, Paris and Padua. She admired the quiet perseverance of the Benedictine Fathers whose stupendous labors in copying out by hand whole manuscripts preserved for moderns the best wisdom of the ancients and thereby more than illuminated an age which is falsely called "dark." She called attention to the wisdom of God in working a miracle of grace in the learned bishop of Hippo and then guiding him on to become the Doctor of Grace. She went out to meet the hordes of Attila at the gates of Rome armed with the "sword of the spirit which is the word of God." She was present when the blood-drenched sands of the Colosseum witnessed how firmly her doctrines could grip the minds of men. She approved a Cyprian when he wrote that we cannot have God as our Father unless we have the Church as our Mother. She bade her erudite son, Origen, to answer the anti-Christian slanders of a sneering Celsus. She knew that the vehement ardor and severe reasoning of a Paul of Tarsus was the "foolishness" that would confound the "wise" who listened to him at the Areopagus of Athens. She knew that only to her did Christ say that she was "a chosen vessel to carry my name among nations."

Wherever there are people to be taught and ignorance to be dispelled, the Church will be found tirelessly working to carry out Christ's mandate. And when the day of reckoning shall at last come and "when the flock shall all be told and the number fulfilled and the shepherds gathered round the Great Shepherd of the sheep in the fold upon the everlasting hills," the Church, asked how she has acquitted herself of her charge, will say, "I was an eye to the blind, a leg to the lame and a father to the poor."

Bibliography

A Catholic Commentary on Holy Scripture. New York: Thomas Nelson and Sons, 1953.

A Treasury of Early Christianity, ed. Anne Fremantle. New York: Viking Press, 1953.

Allard. *Ten Lectures on the Martyrs.* Trans. by Cappadelta. New York: Benziger Bros., Inc., 1907.

Allnatt. *Cathedra Petri.* London: Burns, Oates & Washbourne, 1879.

Aquinas, St. Thomas. *Summa Theologica.* 3 vols. Trans. by English Dominicans. New York: Benziger Bros., Inc., 1947.

Batiffol. *The Credibility of the Gospels.* Trans. by Pollen. London: Longmans, Green & Co., 1912.

Brunsmann-Preuss. *Handbook of Fundamental Theology.* 4 vols. St. Louis: B. Herder Book Co., 1931.

Cayre. *Manual of Patrology.* 2 vols. Trans. by Howitt. Tournai: Descles & Co., 1936.

Davis, Henry, S.J. *Moral and Pastoral Theology.* 4 vols. (4th ed.). London: Sheed & Ward, 1945.

De Grandmaison. *Jesus Christ.* 3 vols. New York: Sheed & Ward, 1934.

Felder. *Christ and the Critics.* Trans. by Stoddard. London: Burns, Oates & Washbourne, 1924.

Gallina. *I Martiri Dei Primi Secoli.* Florence: Salani, 1942.

Garrigou-Lagrange. *The One God.* Trans. by Dom Bede Rose. St. Louis: B. Herder Book Co., 1943.

Grossi-Condi. *I Monumenti Cristiana.* Rome: Gregorian University Press, 1923.

Joyce, G. H. *Principles of Natural Theology.* London: Longmans, Green & Co., 1923.

Joyce, G. H. *The Question of Miracles.* St. Louis: B. Herder Book Co., 1914.

Kenyon. *Our Bible and the Ancient Manuscripts.* New York: Harper & Bros., 1941.

Knox, Ronald. *Enthusiasm.* Oxford: Oxford University Press, 1950.

Lagrange. *The Meaning of Christianity.* Trans. by Reith. New York, 1920.

Lebreton-Zeiller. *History of the Primitive Church.* 2 vols. New York: Macmillan Co., 1944.

Lindsay. *Evidence for the Papacy.* London: Longmans, Green & Co., 1870.

Marucchi. *Manual of Christian Archeology.* Trans. by Vecchierello. Paterson: St. Anthony Guild Press, 1935.

Newman, J. H. *Essays on Miracles.* London: Longmans, Green & Co., 1923.

Otten. *Manual of History of Dogmas.* 2 vols. St. Louis: B. Herder Book Co., 1925.

Phillips. *Modern Thomistic Philosophy.* 2 vols. London: Burns, Oates & Washbourne, 1933.

Prat. *The Theology of St. Paul.* 2 vols. Trans. by Stoddard. London: Burns, Oates & Washbourne, 1942.

Robertson. *Textual Criticism of the New Testament.* London: Hodder & Staughton Ltd., 1925.

Scott, S. H. *The Eastern Churches and the Papacy.* London: Sheed & Ward, 1928.

Studies in Comparative Religion. London: Catholic Truth Society Press.

Tixeront. *History of Dogma.* 3 vols. (3rd ed.). St. Louis: B. Herder Book Co., 1930.

Walshe. *Principles of Catholic Apologetics.* London: Sands & Co., 1926.

Zapelena. *De Ecclesia Christi.* Rome: Gregorian University Press, 1932.

INDEX

Index of Proper Names

Index of Subjects